THE GREAT OUTDOORS

A NATURE BUCKET LIST JOURNAL

LISA T.E. SONNE

ILLUSTRATED BY DICK VINCENT

ROCK
POINT

Artwork © 2016 Dick Vincent
Text © 2016 Quarto Publishing Group USA Inc.
Book design by Tara Long

Hawthorne, Nathaniel. (2012). *The Oxford Book of American Essays*.
  Urbana, Illinois: Project Gutenberg. Retrieved November 11, 2015,
  from Gutenberg.org/eBooks/40196
Muir, John. (2010). *My First Summer in the Sierra*. Urbana, Illinois: Project
  Gutenberg. Retrieved November 11, 2015, from Gutenberg.org/eBooks/32540
Thoreau, Henry David. (1995). *Walden, and On the Duty of Civil Disobedience*.
  Urbana, Illinois: Project Gutenberg. Retrieved November 11, 2015,
  from Gutenberg.org/eBooks/205

First published in the United States of America in 2016 by
Rock Point, a member of
Quarto Publishing Group USA Inc.
142 West 36th Street, 4th Floor
New York, NY 10018

quartoknows.com

10 9 8 7 6 5 4 3 2 1

ISBN: 978-1-63106-234-6

Print in China

🌿 THE GREAT OUTDOORS 🌿
PASSAGES AND PAGES

PRELUDE

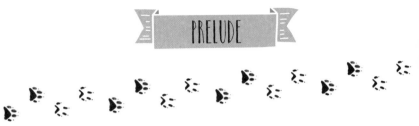

THE GREAT OUTDOORS CALLS and howls and sings and wind-whispers! Can you hear it? It smells of ocean splashes and pungent pines, smoky camp-fires and blooming jasmine. It feels like sand between your toes, textured breezes, and infinity.

The great outdoors is about aliveness, grand and tiny—its fortitude and fragility, its engaging beauty and vital challenge. This journal is about your aliveness—from sublime awe to adrenaline-rush wow.

What do you want to do, see, hear, taste, feel, and smell? What experiences do you want to deposit in the great bank account of your life's memories?

Have you felt a waterfall massage your back? Seen streaks of light shoot across the night sky? Caught snowflakes in your mouth? Summited a mountain and experienced views that change you?

Have you taken a nap at the base of a tree that was alive when your great, great grandparents were? When is the last time you watched clouds? Or did something you have never done before, pushing your physical and mental limits?

Have you rock-climbed, swum, kayaked, zip-lined, hiked? Do you want to?

Have you met deserts, jungles, tundras, and icebergs, and gotten to know them? What would you rather do outdoors? The questions we ask ourselves can get us closer to living the answers we love.

This is your journal for your own inspiration, planning, recording, and remembering so you can enjoy the great outdoors more while you are there! And you can enjoy the great outdoors later, when you are indoors.

Allow yourself to look up at redwoods and stars and gliding egrets. Look out at migrating zebras, bear cubs chewing grasses, glaciers calving, or undulating hills of orange poppies and purple lupine.

And look within. Consider the reflections in your mind as you watch reflections in a meadow pond; the thoughts that settle in your mind when you turn off your flashlight in a cave; the rushes of river rafting.

And then there's the pulling-in and sharing-back what is great about the outdoors in the traditions of scribbling nature-lovers, from Thoreau to John Muir to Nathaniel Hawthorne.

Or you may just want somewhere to gather your bragging rights of mountains and fears conquered, to have a practical place to list all the animals you have seen in the wild, and to keep track of what you really want on your bucket lists.

The rest of this journal has blanks for you to bust out your bucket list, to record your graces and guffaws, or just to doodle. Whether you want to be doing, being, or remembering more, there are pages here for *your* nature in the nature of the world.

TAKE A HIKE

GOOD FOR THE MIND, BODY AND SOUL, hiking is one of the best ways to immerse yourself in the great outdoors. Hikes are entertaining exercise, personal expeditions of exploration, and full of wonders. What are your favorites so far? What do your trail-mates say you should not miss?

What makes a great hike can depend on your hiking companions, the time of year, the weather, how you slept and what you ate, your health, the level of difficulty, and whether the views spoke to you (or talked back to you).

What's your bucket list for where you want your feet to wander and your spirit to wonder? Below are some eclectic ideas to get your mind going on your list. Do you want easy or hard? Short or long? Beach or forest? There is room for you to record your top destinations.

For additional ideas, consider what activities you enjoy (page 36) and what features you want to explore (page 40); whether you want to see specific animals (page 72), birds (page 148), or collections of trees and flowers from around the world (page 140). National parks in many countries offer remarkable hikes (page 120) through beautiful ecosystems, where you can see outstanding features.

TAKE A HIKE

Here is a wonderful list of places to inspire your own list. Research these places and learn more about the amazing things to see when you walk these trails.

ADD TO
BUCKET LIST

DATE
COMPLETED

Harding Icefield Trail, Kenai Fiords, AK

Havasupai-Havasu Canyon and Falls, Grand Canyon, AZ

Sycamore Canyon Wilderness near Cottonwood, AZ

Eastern Sierras, CA

John Muir Trail from Yosemite to Mt. Whitney, CA

Redwood Canyon Trail – Sequoia/Kings Canyon National Park, CA

Tahoe Rim Trail, CA

Diamond Head Summit Trail, Oahu, HI

Electric Peak, Yellowstone, MT (A challenge!)

Lake Sioux Charley in the Beartooth Mountains, MT

Glacier National Park, MT

White Mountain National Forest, NH

Rainbow Falls, OR

Black Hills, SD

Hayduke Trail, UT

Caramount Trail, VT

Bunsen Peak Hike, Yellowstone, WY

Cirque of the Towers, Wind River Range, WY

Burgess Shale in Yoho and Kootenay National Parks, Canada

Edith Cavell Meadows in Jasper National Park, Alberta, Canada

The Skyline Trail in Cape Breton Highlands National Park, Canada

Tablelands in Gros Morne Park, Canada

The West Coast Trail in Pacific Rim National Park Reserve, Canada

HIKING THE WORLD

DO YOU WANT TO HIKE ICONIC PLACES like the Great Wall of China? Mt. Fuji in Japan? The Matterhorn in Switzerland? Ayers Rock in Australia?

There are pilgrimage hikes, like the Nakasendo Way in Japan that weaves through forests from temple to temple, connecting Kyoto and Tokyo since feudal days. The hike to the Tiger's Nest in the Royal Kingdom of Bhutan hugs cliffs and waterfalls to arrive at a temple where it is believed Buddhism started.

You could give your tongue a hike saying you want to hike the Fimmvörðuháls between Eyjafjallajökull glacier and Mýrdalsjökull glacier, one of many great hikes in Iceland. Or you can take the long view on the Long Pathway (Te Araroa) in New Zealand, venturing about 2,700 kilometers from tip to tip of the eye-candy isle.

You can give Siberia a good rap, if you stride the Great Baikal Trail, around the world's oldest, and deepest lake. If you trek in the Vladivostok area of Russia, you might see wild tigers. In China, the Tiger Leaping Gorge is a favorite for the scenery, and Mount Kailash Kora in the Tibetan region is world-class. The Dolomites in Italy and Cappadocia in Turkey are among the globe's geological passages of wonder. Websites, lists, apps, hiking clubs, and walking tour companies all have recommendations...but what do *you* want?

A JOURNEY CAN BEGIN
WITH A SINGLE STEP OR A LINE
IN YOUR JOURNAL

NAME & LOCATION ....

DESCRIPTION ....

....

....

WHERE I HEARD ABOUT IT ....

DATE COMPLETED ..../......./.........

NAME & LOCATION ....

DESCRIPTION ....

....

....

WHERE I HEARD ABOUT IT ....

DATE COMPLETED ..../......./.........

MY BUCKET LIST of HIKES

NAME & LOCATION ....

DESCRIPTION ....

....

....

....

WHERE I HEARD ABOUT IT ....

DATE COMPLETED ..../......./.........

NAME & LOCATION ....

DESCRIPTION ....

....

....

....

WHERE I HEARD ABOUT IT ....

DATE COMPLETED ..../......./.........

NAME & LOCATION ....

DESCRIPTION ....

....

....

....

WHERE I HEARD ABOUT IT ....

DATE COMPLETED ..../......./.........

MY BUCKET LIST of HIKES

NAME & LOCATION

DESCRIPTION

WHERE I HEARD ABOUT IT

DATE COMPLETED _____ / _____ / _____

NAME & LOCATION

DESCRIPTION

WHERE I HEARD ABOUT IT

DATE COMPLETED _____ / _____ / _____

NAME & LOCATION

DESCRIPTION

WHERE I HEARD ABOUT IT

DATE COMPLETED _____ / _____ / _____

THE WINNERS

Golf has evolved from a sedate pastime to a nationally recognized sport. Professional golfers on the tour compete for high honors—and for high stakes. Just for the record, this list shows the leading money-maker in each year since 1934, and the dollar amount that put each golfer at the top.

TOP MONEY-MAKERS

1934	Paul Runyan	$6,767	1947	Jimmy Demaret	$27,936
1935	Johnny Revolta	$9,543	1948	Ben Hogan	$32,112
1936	Horton Smith	$7,682	1949	Sam Snead	$31,593
1937	Harry Cooper	$14,138	1950	Sam Snead	$35,758
1938	Sam Snead	$19,534	1951	Lloyd Mangrum	$26,088
1939	Henry Picard	$10,303	1952	Julius Boros	$37,032
1940	Ben Hogan	$10,655	1953	Lew Worsham	$34,002
1941	Ben Hogan	$18,358	1954	Bob Toski	$65,819
1942	Ben Hogan	$13,143	1955	Julius Boros	$63,121
1943	No statistics compiled		1956	Ted Kroll	$72,835
1944	Byron Nelson	$37,967	1957	Dick Mayer	$65,835
1945	Byron Nelson	$63,335	1958	Arnold Palmer	$42,607
1946	Ben Hogan	$42,556	1959	Art Wall	$53,167

1960	Arnold Palmer	$75,262	1977	Tom Watson	$310,653
1961	Gary Player	$64,540	1978	Tom Watson	$362,428
1962	Arnold Palmer	$81,448	1979	Tom Watson	$462,635
1963	Arnold Palmer	$128,230	1980	Tom Watson	$530,808
1964	Jack Nicklaus	$113,284	1981	Tom Kite	$375,698
1965	Jack Nicklaus	$140,752	1982	Craig Sladler	$446,462
1966	Billy Casper	$121,944	1983	Hal Sutton	$426,668
1967	Jack Nicklaus	$188,998	1984	Tom Watson	$476,260
1968	Billy Casper	$205,168	1985	Curtis Strange	$542,321
1969	Frank Beard	$164,707	1986	Greg Norman	$653,296
1970	Lee Trevino	$157,037	1987	Curtis Strange	$925,941
1971	Jack Nicklaus	$244,490	1988	Curtis Strange	$1,147,644
1972	Jack Nicklaus	$320,542	1989	Tom Kite	$1,395,278
1973	Jack Nicklaus	$308,362	1990	Greg Norman	$1,165,477
1974	Johnny Miller	$353,021	1991	Corey Pavin	$979,430
1975	Jack Nicklaus	$298,149	1992	Fred Couples	$1,344,188
1976	Jack Nicklaus	$266,438			

MY BUCKET LIST of HIKES

NAME & LOCATION ....

DESCRIPTION ....

....

....

....

WHERE I HEARD ABOUT IT ....

DATE COMPLETED ..... / ..... / ....

NAME & LOCATION ....

DESCRIPTION ....

....

....

....

WHERE I HEARD ABOUT IT ....

DATE COMPLETED ..... / ..... / ....

NAME & LOCATION ....

DESCRIPTION ....

....

....

....

WHERE I HEARD ABOUT IT ....

DATE COMPLETED ..... / ..... / ....

MY BUCKET LIST of HIKES

NAME & LOCATION ....

DESCRIPTION ....

....

....

....

WHERE I HEARD ABOUT IT ....

DATE COMPLETED .... / .... / ....

NAME & LOCATION ....

DESCRIPTION ....

....

....

....

WHERE I HEARD ABOUT IT ....

DATE COMPLETED .... / .... / ....

NAME & LOCATION ....

DESCRIPTION ....

....

....

....

WHERE I HEARD ABOUT IT ....

DATE COMPLETED .... / .... / ....

MY BUCKET LIST of HIKES

NAME & LOCATION ....

DESCRIPTION ....

....

....

....

WHERE I HEARD ABOUT IT ....

DATE COMPLETED .... / .... / ....

NAME & LOCATION ....

DESCRIPTION ....

....

....

....

WHERE I HEARD ABOUT IT ....

DATE COMPLETED .... / .... / ....

NAME & LOCATION ....

DESCRIPTION ....

....

....

....

WHERE I HEARD ABOUT IT ....

DATE COMPLETED .... / .... / ....

MY BUCKET LIST OF HIKES

NAME & LOCATION ....

DESCRIPTION ....

....

....

....

WHERE I HEARD ABOUT IT ....

DATE COMPLETED ..../ ..../ ....

NAME & LOCATION ....

DESCRIPTION ....

....

....

....

WHERE I HEARD ABOUT IT ....

DATE COMPLETED ..../ ..../ ....

NAME & LOCATION ....

DESCRIPTION ....

....

....

....

WHERE I HEARD ABOUT IT ....

DATE COMPLETED ..../ ..../ ....

MY BUCKET LIST OF HIKES

NAME & LOCATION

DESCRIPTION

WHERE I HEARD ABOUT IT

DATE COMPLETED _____ / _____ / _____

NAME & LOCATION

DESCRIPTION

WHERE I HEARD ABOUT IT

DATE COMPLETED _____ / _____ / _____

NAME & LOCATION

DESCRIPTION

WHERE I HEARD ABOUT IT

DATE COMPLETED _____ / _____ / _____

MY BUCKET LIST of HIKES

NAME & LOCATION ....

DESCRIPTION ....

....

....

....

WHERE I HEARD ABOUT IT ....

DATE COMPLETED ..../......./...........

NAME & LOCATION ....

DESCRIPTION ....

....

....

....

WHERE I HEARD ABOUT IT ....

DATE COMPLETED ..../......./...........

NAME & LOCATION ....

DESCRIPTION ....

....

....

....

WHERE I HEARD ABOUT IT ....

DATE COMPLETED ..../......./...........

MY BUCKET LIST OF HIKES

NAME & LOCATION ....

DESCRIPTION ....

....

....

....

WHERE I HEARD ABOUT IT ....

DATE COMPLETED .... / .... / ....

NAME & LOCATION ....

DESCRIPTION ....

....

....

....

WHERE I HEARD ABOUT IT ....

DATE COMPLETED .... / .... / ....

NAME & LOCATION ....

DESCRIPTION ....

....

....

....

WHERE I HEARD ABOUT IT ....

DATE COMPLETED .... / .... / ....

MY BUCKET LIST OF HIKES

NAME & LOCATION ....

DESCRIPTION ....

....

....

....

WHERE I HEARD ABOUT IT ....

DATE COMPLETED .... / .... / ....

NAME & LOCATION ....

DESCRIPTION ....

....

....

....

WHERE I HEARD ABOUT IT ....

DATE COMPLETED .... / .... / ....

NAME & LOCATION ....

DESCRIPTION ....

....

....

....

WHERE I HEARD ABOUT IT ....

DATE COMPLETED .... / .... / ....

MY BUCKET LIST of HIKES

NAME & LOCATION ....

DESCRIPTION ....

....

....

....

WHERE I HEARD ABOUT IT ....

DATE COMPLETED .... / .... / ....

NAME & LOCATION ....

DESCRIPTION ....

....

....

....

WHERE I HEARD ABOUT IT ....

DATE COMPLETED .... / .... / ....

NAME & LOCATION ....

DESCRIPTION ....

....

....

....

WHERE I HEARD ABOUT IT ....

DATE COMPLETED .... / .... / ....

MY BUCKET LIST of HIKES

NAME & LOCATION ....

DESCRIPTION ....

....

....

....

WHERE I HEARD ABOUT IT ....

DATE COMPLETED ....../....../......

NAME & LOCATION ....

DESCRIPTION ....

....

....

....

WHERE I HEARD ABOUT IT ....

DATE COMPLETED ....../....../......

NAME & LOCATION ....

DESCRIPTION ....

....

....

....

WHERE I HEARD ABOUT IT ....

DATE COMPLETED ....../....../......

MY BUCKET LIST of HIKES

NAME & LOCATION ....

DESCRIPTION ....

....

....

....

WHERE I HEARD ABOUT IT ....

DATE COMPLETED ..../......../........

NAME & LOCATION ....

DESCRIPTION ....

....

....

....

WHERE I HEARD ABOUT IT ....

DATE COMPLETED ..../......../........

NAME & LOCATION ....

DESCRIPTION ....

....

....

....

WHERE I HEARD ABOUT IT ....

DATE COMPLETED ..../......../........

MY BUCKET LIST of HIKES

NAME & LOCATION ....

DESCRIPTION ....

....

....

....

WHERE I HEARD ABOUT IT ....

DATE COMPLETED .... / .... / ....

NAME & LOCATION ....

DESCRIPTION ....

....

....

....

WHERE I HEARD ABOUT IT ....

DATE COMPLETED .... / .... / ....

NAME & LOCATION ....

DESCRIPTION ....

....

....

....

WHERE I HEARD ABOUT IT ....

DATE COMPLETED .... / .... / ....

MY BUCKET LIST OF HIKES

NAME & LOCATION ....

DESCRIPTION ....

....

....

....

WHERE I HEARD ABOUT IT ....

DATE COMPLETED ..../......./.........

NAME & LOCATION ....

DESCRIPTION ....

....

....

....

WHERE I HEARD ABOUT IT ....

DATE COMPLETED ..../......./.........

NAME & LOCATION ....

DESCRIPTION ....

....

....

....

WHERE I HEARD ABOUT IT ....

DATE COMPLETED ..../......./.........

MY BUCKET LIST of HIKES

NAME & LOCATION ....

DESCRIPTION ....

....

....

....

WHERE I HEARD ABOUT IT ....

DATE COMPLETED .... / .... / ....

NAME & LOCATION ....

DESCRIPTION ....

....

....

....

WHERE I HEARD ABOUT IT ....

DATE COMPLETED .... / .... / ....

NAME & LOCATION ....

DESCRIPTION ....

....

....

....

WHERE I HEARD ABOUT IT ....

DATE COMPLETED .... / .... / ....

MY BUCKET LIST of HIKES

NAME & LOCATION ....

DESCRIPTION ....

....

....

....

WHERE I HEARD ABOUT IT ....

DATE COMPLETED ..../......../........

NAME & LOCATION ....

DESCRIPTION ....

....

....

....

WHERE I HEARD ABOUT IT ....

DATE COMPLETED ..../......../........

NAME & LOCATION ....

DESCRIPTION ....

....

....

....

WHERE I HEARD ABOUT IT ....

DATE COMPLETED ..../......../........

MY BUCKET LIST OF HIKES

NAME & LOCATION ....

DESCRIPTION ....

....

....

....

WHERE I HEARD ABOUT IT ....

DATE COMPLETED .... / .... / ....

NAME & LOCATION ....

DESCRIPTION ....

....

....

....

WHERE I HEARD ABOUT IT ....

DATE COMPLETED .... / .... / ....

NAME & LOCATION ....

DESCRIPTION ....

....

....

....

WHERE I HEARD ABOUT IT ....

DATE COMPLETED .... / .... / ....

MY BUCKET LIST of HIKES

NAME & LOCATION ....

DESCRIPTION ....

....

....

....

WHERE I HEARD ABOUT IT ....

DATE COMPLETED .... / .... / ....

NAME & LOCATION ....

DESCRIPTION ....

....

....

....

WHERE I HEARD ABOUT IT ....

DATE COMPLETED .... / .... / ....

NAME & LOCATION ....

DESCRIPTION ....

....

....

....

WHERE I HEARD ABOUT IT ....

DATE COMPLETED .... / .... / ....

AMAZING GEOGRAPHICAL FEATURES

THE WORLD IS FULL OF AMAZING NATURAL WONDERS. More than features on a topographical map, these places should be explored and always included in a nature lover's bucket list.

Explore a glacier, hike an iceberg, or swim under a waterfall. Do you want to walk behind part of the largest waterfall in North America? Try the Horseshoe Falls portion of Niagara Falls. Do you want to sing behind a waterfall that is inside a cave? One place you can go is Ruby Falls in Tennessee, romantically named by the discoverer for his wife, Ruby. Waterfalls around the world can offer swimming pools, sacred sites, natural water slides, and gorgeous photo ops.

GET OUT THERE AND EXPLORE!

Listed below the are some amazing geographical features to help you plan your adventures.

	ADD TO BUCKET LIST	WHERE	WHEN
Archipelago			
Arch			
Bay			
Bog			
Blowhole			
Caldera			
Canyon			
Cape			
Cave			
Cavern			
Cliff			
Coral Reef			
Delta			
Desert			
Dune			
Estuary			
Fjord			
Forest			
Geyser			
Glacier			
Grotto			
Gulf			
Hoodoo (Fairy Chimney)			
Hot Spring			
Iceberg			
Island			
Jungle			
Karst			

	ADD TO BUCKET LIST	WHERE	WHEN
Lagoon			
Lava Tube			
Loch			
Meadow			
Mesa			
Monolith			
Mountain			
Peninsula			
Pingo			
Pond			
Pool (Natural)			
Plain			
Plateau			
Prairie			
Rainforest			
Range			
Salt Flats			
Savannah			
Sea			
Slough			
Strait			
Swamp			
Tufa			
Tundra			
Valley			
Volcano			
Waterfall			
Wetland			
Woodland			

WOW EXPERIENCES

THE GREAT OUTDOORS offer some very pretty places that also have some pretty amazing phenomena of nature. Here's a start for some bucket-list Wow Experiences. What do you want to add to your life?

ADD TO
BUCKET LIST

Paddle with glowworms in bioluminescent waters.

See synchronous fireflies as they flash on and off in the dark.

Soak in hot mineral springs with spectacular vistas.

Witness at least one great migration of creatures (the monarch butterflies, humpback whales, Sandhill cranes, or the zebras and wildebeests).

See the sun rise and set in the same five-minute period, by heading toward the Arctic or Antarctic Circle during a solstice—the days (in winter) or the nights (in summer) can be only a few minutes long.

WHALE WATCHING

Feel pink sand between your toes.

Enjoy the weird lights of glowworms in one of dozens of caves worldwide.

Experience the darkest dark by standing deep in a cave and turning off all the lights.

Come eye-to-eye with a whale shark while snorkeling.

Seek a moonbo—a rainbow at night formed from moonlight hitting certain waterfalls just right.

Witness the light dance of the Northern Lights (Aurora Borealis) or the Southern Lights (Aurora Australis).

See the fires and the lava-flow paths of a volcano.

Enjoy a double rainbow.

Pick a mango fresh from a tree and eat it.

Gander at a geyser gushing upward.

See the green flash of a sunset.

Witness a coral spawn.

Be the only human in a meadow of splendiferous wildflowers, a perfumery of Spring.

THERE IS ALWAYS MORE TO ADD
TO THE BUCKET LIST OF WOW EXPERIENCES!

*To write about your wow experiences, there are pages for your passages
in the back of this journal.*

MY ADVENTURES

FROM ASH—BOARDING DOWN A VOLCANO to zip-lining through the canopy of a tropical forest, outdoor activities can pump your muscles, mood, and memories. Back in the day, canoeing, kayaking, hiking, horseback riding, dog sledding, skiing, and river rafting were all practical modes of transportation.

You may be looking for adrenaline, or you may want a different perspective on the landscape. If so, go aerial with kite-boarding, zip-lining, or parasailing. You may want to go underground or underwater with caving and snorkeling or diving. Remember to check with your doctor first if you have any health concerns, and make safety a priority so you have more years to fill your bucket of life experiences.

Modern, outdoor yoga is gaining popularity, from the beaches of Malibu to remote retreats, for those who want to breathe outdoor air deeply and meditate without ceilings.

Peruse this amazing list of fun and adventurous activities that let you move through the great outdoors while being moved by beauty.

ADVENTURE STARTS HERE

MY ADVENTURE STARTER LIST

	ADD TO BUCKET LIST	ACCOMPLISHED	WHERE	WHEN
Ash-boarding				
Backpacking				
Biking				
Birding				
Camping				
Canoeing				
Caving				
Cloud-gazing				
Dog sledging				
Fly fishing				
Geo-caching				
Gliding				
Golfing				
Hang-gliding				
Hiking				
Horseback riding				
Kayaking				
Kite-boarding				

MY ADVENTURE STARTER LIST

	ADD TO BUCKET LIST	ACCOMPLISHED	WHERE	WHEN
Outdoor yoga				
Paddle-boarding				
Parasailing				
River rafting				
Rock climbing				
Rock collecting				
Sailing				
Scuba diving				
Snorkeling				
Snowboarding				
Snowshoeing				
Stargazing				
Surfing				
Tree climbing				
Trekking				
Windsurfing				
Zip-lining				

MY OUTDOOR ADVENTURE BUCKET LIST

ADVENTURE ....
LOCATION ....
WHAT DO I NEED TO PREPARE ....

....
WHY? ....

....
DATE COMPLETED .... / .... / ....

ADVENTURE ....
LOCATION ....
WHAT DO I NEED TO PREPARE ....

....
WHY? ....

....
DATE COMPLETED .... / .... / ....

ADVENTURE ....
LOCATION ....
WHAT DO I NEED TO PREPARE ....

....
WHY? ....

....
DATE COMPLETED .... / .... / ....

MY OUTDOOR ADVENTURE BUCKET LIST

ADVENTURE ....

LOCATION ....

WHAT DO I NEED TO PREPARE ....

....

WHY? ....

....

DATE COMPLETED ....../....../..........

ADVENTURE ....

LOCATION ....

WHAT DO I NEED TO PREPARE ....

....

WHY? ....

....

DATE COMPLETED ....../....../..........

ADVENTURE ....

LOCATION ....

WHAT DO I NEED TO PREPARE ....

....

WHY? ....

....

DATE COMPLETED ....../....../..........

MY OUTDOOR ADVENTURE BUCKET LIST

ADVENTURE ....
LOCATION ....
WHAT DO I NEED TO PREPARE ....

....

WHY? ....

....

DATE COMPLETED .... / .... / ....

ADVENTURE ....
LOCATION ....
WHAT DO I NEED TO PREPARE ....

....

WHY? ....

....

DATE COMPLETED .... / .... / ....

ADVENTURE ....
LOCATION ....
WHAT DO I NEED TO PREPARE ....

....

WHY? ....

....

DATE COMPLETED .... / .... / ....

MY OUTDOOR ADVENTURE BUCKET LIST

ADVENTURE ....
LOCATION ....
WHAT DO I NEED TO PREPARE ....

....
WHY? ....

....
DATE COMPLETED ...... / ...... / ....

ADVENTURE ....
LOCATION ....
WHAT DO I NEED TO PREPARE ....

....
WHY? ....

....
DATE COMPLETED ...... / ...... / ....

ADVENTURE ....
LOCATION ....
WHAT DO I NEED TO PREPARE ....

....
WHY? ....

....
DATE COMPLETED ...... / ...... / ....

MY OUTDOOR ADVENTURE BUCKET LIST

ADVENTURE ....
LOCATION ....
WHAT DO I NEED TO PREPARE ....
....
WHY? ....
....
DATE COMPLETED ..../......./.........

ADVENTURE ....
LOCATION ....
WHAT DO I NEED TO PREPARE ....
....
WHY? ....
....
DATE COMPLETED ..../......./.........

ADVENTURE ....
LOCATION ....
WHAT DO I NEED TO PREPARE ....
....
WHY? ....
....
DATE COMPLETED ..../......./.........

MY OUTDOOR ADVENTURE BUCKET LIST

ADVENTURE --
LOCATION ---
WHAT DO I NEED TO PREPARE --

WHY? ---

DATE COMPLETED ------ / ------ / --------

ADVENTURE --
LOCATION ---
WHAT DO I NEED TO PREPARE --

WHY? ---

DATE COMPLETED ------ / ------ / --------

ADVENTURE --
LOCATION ---
WHAT DO I NEED TO PREPARE --

WHY? ---

DATE COMPLETED ------ / ------ / --------

MY OUTDOOR ADVENTURE BUCKET LIST

ADVENTURE ....
LOCATION ....
WHAT DO I NEED TO PREPARE ....

....

WHY? ....

....

DATE COMPLETED .... / .... / ....

ADVENTURE ....
LOCATION ....
WHAT DO I NEED TO PREPARE ....

....

WHY? ....

....

DATE COMPLETED .... / .... / ....

ADVENTURE ....
LOCATION ....
WHAT DO I NEED TO PREPARE ....

....

WHY? ....

....

DATE COMPLETED .... / .... / ....

MY OUTDOOR ADVENTURE BUCKET LIST

ADVENTURE ....
LOCATION ....
WHAT DO I NEED TO PREPARE ....
....
WHY? ....
....
DATE COMPLETED .... / .... / ....

ADVENTURE ....
LOCATION ....
WHAT DO I NEED TO PREPARE ....
....
WHY? ....
....
DATE COMPLETED .... / .... / ....

ADVENTURE ....
LOCATION ....
WHAT DO I NEED TO PREPARE ....
....
WHY? ....
....
DATE COMPLETED .... / .... / ....

MY OUTDOOR ADVENTURE BUCKET LIST

ADVENTURE ....
LOCATION ....
WHAT DO I NEED TO PREPARE ....
....
WHY? ....
....
DATE COMPLETED ..../......./........

ADVENTURE ....
LOCATION ....
WHAT DO I NEED TO PREPARE ....
....
WHY? ....
....
DATE COMPLETED ..../......./........

ADVENTURE ....
LOCATION ....
WHAT DO I NEED TO PREPARE ....
....
WHY? ....
....
DATE COMPLETED ..../......./........

MY OUTDOOR ADVENTURE BUCKET LIST

ADVENTURE ....
LOCATION ....
WHAT DO I NEED TO PREPARE ....
....
WHY? ....
....
DATE COMPLETED .... / ...... / ....

ADVENTURE ....
LOCATION ....
WHAT DO I NEED TO PREPARE ....
....
WHY? ....
....
DATE COMPLETED .... / ...... / ....

ADVENTURE ....
LOCATION ....
WHAT DO I NEED TO PREPARE ....
....
WHY? ....
....
DATE COMPLETED .... / ...... / ....

MY OUTDOOR ADVENTURE BUCKET LIST

ADVENTURE ....
LOCATION ....
WHAT DO I NEED TO PREPARE ....
....
WHY? ....
....
DATE COMPLETED .... / .... / ....

ADVENTURE ....
LOCATION ....
WHAT DO I NEED TO PREPARE ....
....
WHY? ....
....
DATE COMPLETED .... / .... / ....

ADVENTURE ....
LOCATION ....
WHAT DO I NEED TO PREPARE ....
....
WHY? ....
....
DATE COMPLETED .... / .... / ....

MY OUTDOOR ADVENTURE BUCKET LIST

ADVENTURE
LOCATION
WHAT DO I NEED TO PREPARE

WHY?

DATE COMPLETED ____ / ____ / _____

ADVENTURE
LOCATION
WHAT DO I NEED TO PREPARE

WHY?

DATE COMPLETED ____ / ____ / _____

ADVENTURE
LOCATION
WHAT DO I NEED TO PREPARE

WHY?

DATE COMPLETED ____ / ____ / _____

THE JOY OF CAMPING
DREAMING UNDER THE STARS

HOW DO YOU SPEND THAT "THIRD OF YOUR LIFE SLEEPING" when you are on trips to enjoy the great outdoors?

Do you assemble your favorite tent at great camping spots? Are you a car-camper? Or have you backpacked into stellar spots? Do you research the best lodges with cabins in the woods or balconies facing the sea? Maybe you relish being with Mother Nature in more novel ways—staying in tree-houses or ice hotels. There are even underwater rooms available and cave rooms—from the troglodyte dwellings of the Cappadocia region of Turkey, to a *literally* cavernous, modern room in the Grand Canyon Caverns with an elevator to take you back up the equivalent of more than twenty stories.

Where do you want to rest your head?

THE
JOY of CAMPING

DREAM PLACES FOR CAMPING IN THE GREAT OUTDOORS

NAME ....

LOCATION ....

TYPE OF PLACE ....

NOTES ....

....

DATE COMPLETED .... / .... / ....

NAME ....

LOCATION ....

TYPE OF PLACE ....

NOTES ....

....

DATE COMPLETED .... / .... / ....

NAME ....

LOCATION ....

TYPE OF PLACE ....

NOTES ....

....

DATE COMPLETED .... / .... / ....

DREAM PLACES FOR CAMPING IN THE GREAT OUTDOORS

NAME ....

LOCATION ....

TYPE OF PLACE ....

NOTES ....

....

....

DATE COMPLETED .... / .... / ....

NAME ....

LOCATION ....

TYPE OF PLACE ....

NOTES ....

....

....

DATE COMPLETED .... / .... / ....

NAME ....

LOCATION ....

TYPE OF PLACE ....

NOTES ....

....

....

DATE COMPLETED .... / .... / ....

DREAM PLACES FOR CAMPING IN THE GREAT OUTDOORS

NAME ....
LOCATION ....
TYPE OF PLACE ....

NOTES ....
....

DATE COMPLETED ..../......./.........

NAME ....
LOCATION ....
TYPE OF PLACE ....

NOTES ....
....

DATE COMPLETED ..../......./.........

NAME ....
LOCATION ....
TYPE OF PLACE ....

NOTES ....
....

DATE COMPLETED ..../......./.........

DREAM PLACES FOR CAMPING IN THE GREAT OUTDOORS

NAME _____
LOCATION _____
TYPE OF PLACE _____

NOTES _____
_____
_____

DATE COMPLETED _____ / _____ / _____

NAME _____
LOCATION _____
TYPE OF PLACE _____

NOTES _____
_____
_____

DATE COMPLETED _____ / _____ / _____

NAME _____
LOCATION _____
TYPE OF PLACE _____

NOTES _____
_____
_____

DATE COMPLETED _____ / _____ / _____

DREAM PLACES FOR CAMPING IN THE GREAT OUTDOORS

NAME ....
LOCATION ....
TYPE OF PLACE ....

NOTES ....
....
....

DATE COMPLETED ...... / ...... / ....

NAME ....
LOCATION ....
TYPE OF PLACE ....

NOTES ....
....
....

DATE COMPLETED ...... / ...... / ....

NAME ....
LOCATION ....
TYPE OF PLACE ....

NOTES ....
....
....

DATE COMPLETED ...... / ...... / ....

DREAM PLACES FOR CAMPING IN THE GREAT OUTDOORS

NAME ....
LOCATION ....
TYPE OF PLACE ....

....

NOTES ....

....

....

DATE COMPLETED ..../......./.........

NAME ....
LOCATION ....
TYPE OF PLACE ....

....

NOTES ....

....

....

DATE COMPLETED ..../......./.........

NAME ....
LOCATION ....
TYPE OF PLACE ....

....

NOTES ....

....

....

DATE COMPLETED ..../......./.........

DREAM PLACES FOR CAMPING IN THE GREAT OUTDOORS

NAME ....
LOCATION ....
TYPE OF PLACE ....

NOTES ....
....
....

DATE COMPLETED ..../......./.........

NAME ....
LOCATION ....
TYPE OF PLACE ....

NOTES ....
....
....

DATE COMPLETED ..../......./.........

NAME ....
LOCATION ....
TYPE OF PLACE ....

NOTES ....
....
....

DATE COMPLETED ..../......./.........

DREAM PLACES FOR CAMPING IN THE GREAT OUTDOORS

NAME ....
LOCATION ....
TYPE OF PLACE ....

NOTES ....
....
....

DATE COMPLETED ....../....../..........

NAME ....
LOCATION ....
TYPE OF PLACE ....

NOTES ....
....
....

DATE COMPLETED ....../....../..........

NAME ....
LOCATION ....
TYPE OF PLACE ....

NOTES ....
....
....

DATE COMPLETED ....../....../..........

DREAM PLACES FOR CAMPING IN THE GREAT OUTDOORS

NAME _____
LOCATION _____
TYPE OF PLACE _____

NOTES _____
_____

DATE COMPLETED _____ / _____ / _____

NAME _____
LOCATION _____
TYPE OF PLACE _____

NOTES _____
_____

DATE COMPLETED _____ / _____ / _____

NAME _____
LOCATION _____
TYPE OF PLACE _____

NOTES _____
_____

DATE COMPLETED _____ / _____ / _____

DREAM PLACES FOR CAMPING IN THE GREAT OUTDOORS

NAME ....
LOCATION ....
TYPE OF PLACE ....

NOTES ....
....
....

DATE COMPLETED ..../......./.........

NAME ....
LOCATION ....
TYPE OF PLACE ....

NOTES ....
....
....

DATE COMPLETED ..../......./.........

NAME ....
LOCATION ....
TYPE OF PLACE ....

NOTES ....
....
....

DATE COMPLETED ..../......./.........

DREAM PLACES FOR CAMPING IN THE GREAT OUTDOORS

NAME ....

LOCATION ....

TYPE OF PLACE ....

NOTES ....

....

....

DATE COMPLETED .... / .... / ....

NAME ....

LOCATION ....

TYPE OF PLACE ....

NOTES ....

....

....

DATE COMPLETED .... / .... / ....

NAME ....

LOCATION ....

TYPE OF PLACE ....

NOTES ....

....

....

DATE COMPLETED .... / .... / ....

DREAM PLACES FOR CAMPING IN THE GREAT OUTDOORS

NAME ....

LOCATION ....

TYPE OF PLACE ....

NOTES ....

....

....

DATE COMPLETED .... / .... / ....

NAME ....

LOCATION ....

TYPE OF PLACE ....

NOTES ....

....

....

DATE COMPLETED .... / .... / ....

NAME ....

LOCATION ....

TYPE OF PLACE ....

NOTES ....

....

....

DATE COMPLETED .... / .... / ....

DREAM PLACES FOR CAMPING IN THE GREAT OUTDOORS

NAME ....
LOCATION ....
TYPE OF PLACE ....

NOTES ....
....
....

DATE COMPLETED .... / .... / ....

NAME ....
LOCATION ....
TYPE OF PLACE ....

NOTES ....
....
....

DATE COMPLETED .... / .... / ....

NAME ....
LOCATION ....
TYPE OF PLACE ....

NOTES ....
....
....

DATE COMPLETED .... / .... / ....

DREAM PLACES FOR CAMPING IN THE GREAT OUTDOORS

NAME ....
LOCATION ....
TYPE OF PLACE ....

NOTES ....
....
....

DATE COMPLETED ..../ ...... / ....

NAME ....
LOCATION ....
TYPE OF PLACE ....

NOTES ....
....
....

DATE COMPLETED ..../ ...... / ....

NAME ....
LOCATION ....
TYPE OF PLACE ....

NOTES ....
....
....

DATE COMPLETED ..../ ...... / ....

WILDLIFE
ALL CREATURES GREAT AND SMALL

WHAT'S ON YOUR WILDLIFE WISH LIST? A wombat? Narwhal? Taiken? Kangaroo? Don't forget the dung beetle or platypus!

Have you heard the songs of the humpback whales while swimming or snorkeling near green sea turtles?

Do you want to see a creature break through an egg and hatch? Maybe a penguin chick, a baby turtle, an albatross, an iguana, a chicken, or an ostrich?

Do you want to collect big-cat sightings? There are so many: lions and tigers and bobcats, as well as cheetahs, cougars, ocelots, leopards, and panthers.

Or are you a primate fan who wants to see baboons, gorillas, orangutans, gibbons, and chimpanzees in their natural habitats?

Do you want to learn to identify the footprints of forest animals and go tracking for badgers or foxes or bears?

Perhaps you want to kiss a giraffe, feed a manatee, hold a three-toed sloth, or brush an elephant. You may want to check out reputable animal sanctuaries and rescue centers in countries you visit.

We humans are only one of more than 7 million species of animals on this planet that includes fishes, birds, and insects. That's a lot of meet-and-greets, if we want to be friendly.

MY BUCKET LIST of WILDLIFE TO SEE

NAME OF ANIMAL ....
WHERE I WANT TO GO TO SEE IT ....
TYPE OF PLACE ....

NOTES ....

DATE SEEN .... / .... / ....

NAME OF ANIMAL ....
WHERE I WANT TO GO TO SEE IT ....
TYPE OF PLACE ....

NOTES ....

DATE SEEN .... / .... / ....

NAME OF ANIMAL ....
WHERE I WANT TO GO TO SEE IT ....
TYPE OF PLACE ....

NOTES ....

DATE SEEN .... / .... / ....

MY BUCKET LIST of WILDLIFE TO SEE

NAME OF ANIMAL

WHERE I WANT TO GO TO SEE IT

TYPE OF PLACE

NOTES

DATE SEEN ...... / ...... / ....

NAME OF ANIMAL

WHERE I WANT TO GO TO SEE IT

TYPE OF PLACE

NOTES

DATE SEEN ...... / ...... / ....

NAME OF ANIMAL

WHERE I WANT TO GO TO SEE IT

TYPE OF PLACE

NOTES

DATE SEEN ...... / ...... / ....

MY BUCKET LIST OF WILDLIFE TO SEE

NAME OF ANIMAL ....

WHERE I WANT TO GO TO SEE IT ....

TYPE OF PLACE ....

....

NOTES ....

....

DATE SEEN .... / .... / ....

NAME OF ANIMAL ....

WHERE I WANT TO GO TO SEE IT ....

TYPE OF PLACE ....

....

NOTES ....

....

DATE SEEN .... / .... / ....

NAME OF ANIMAL ....

WHERE I WANT TO GO TO SEE IT ....

TYPE OF PLACE ....

....

NOTES ....

....

DATE SEEN .... / .... / ....

MY BUCKET LIST of WILDLIFE TO SEE

NAME OF ANIMAL ....
WHERE I WANT TO GO TO SEE IT ....
TYPE OF PLACE ....
....
NOTES ....
....
DATE SEEN .... / .... / ....

NAME OF ANIMAL ....
WHERE I WANT TO GO TO SEE IT ....
TYPE OF PLACE ....
....
NOTES ....
....
DATE SEEN .... / .... / ....

NAME OF ANIMAL ....
WHERE I WANT TO GO TO SEE IT ....
TYPE OF PLACE ....
....
NOTES ....
....
DATE SEEN .... / .... / ....

MY BUCKET LIST of WILDLIFE TO SEE

NAME OF ANIMAL ....
WHERE I WANT TO GO TO SEE IT ....
TYPE OF PLACE ....

NOTES ....

DATE SEEN ..../......./.........

NAME OF ANIMAL ....
WHERE I WANT TO GO TO SEE IT ....
TYPE OF PLACE ....

NOTES ....

DATE SEEN ..../......./.........

NAME OF ANIMAL ....
WHERE I WANT TO GO TO SEE IT ....
TYPE OF PLACE ....

NOTES ....

DATE SEEN ..../......./.........

MY BUCKET LIST of WILDLIFE TO SEE

NAME OF ANIMAL ....
WHERE I WANT TO GO TO SEE IT ....
TYPE OF PLACE ....
....

NOTES ....

....

DATE SEEN .... / .... / ....

NAME OF ANIMAL ....
WHERE I WANT TO GO TO SEE IT ....
TYPE OF PLACE ....
....

NOTES ....

....

DATE SEEN .... / .... / ....

NAME OF ANIMAL ....
WHERE I WANT TO GO TO SEE IT ....
TYPE OF PLACE ....
....

NOTES ....

....

DATE SEEN .... / .... / ....

MY BUCKET LIST OF WILDLIFE TO SEE

NAME OF ANIMAL ....

WHERE I WANT TO GO TO SEE IT ....

TYPE OF PLACE ....

....

NOTES ....

....

DATE SEEN .... / .... / ....

NAME OF ANIMAL ....

WHERE I WANT TO GO TO SEE IT ....

TYPE OF PLACE ....

....

NOTES ....

....

DATE SEEN .... / .... / ....

MY BUCKET LIST of WILDLIFE TO SEE

NAME OF ANIMAL ....

WHERE I WANT TO GO TO SEE IT ....

TYPE OF PLACE ....

NOTES ....

DATE SEEN .... / .... / ....

NAME OF ANIMAL ....

WHERE I WANT TO GO TO SEE IT ....

TYPE OF PLACE ....

NOTES ....

DATE SEEN .... / .... / ....

NAME OF ANIMAL ....

WHERE I WANT TO GO TO SEE IT ....

TYPE OF PLACE ....

NOTES ....

DATE SEEN .... / .... / ....

MY BUCKET LIST OF WILDLIFE TO SEE

NAME OF ANIMAL ....

WHERE I WANT TO GO TO SEE IT ....

TYPE OF PLACE ....

NOTES ....

DATE SEEN ..../......./..........

NAME OF ANIMAL ....

WHERE I WANT TO GO TO SEE IT ....

TYPE OF PLACE ....

NOTES ....

DATE SEEN ..../......./..........

NAME OF ANIMAL ....

WHERE I WANT TO GO TO SEE IT ....

TYPE OF PLACE ....

NOTES ....

DATE SEEN ..../......./..........

MY BUCKET LIST OF WILDLIFE TO SEE

NAME OF ANIMAL ....
WHERE I WANT TO GO TO SEE IT ....
TYPE OF PLACE ....

....
NOTES ....

DATE SEEN ..../......./...........

NAME OF ANIMAL ....
WHERE I WANT TO GO TO SEE IT ....
TYPE OF PLACE ....

....
NOTES ....

DATE SEEN ..../......./...........

NAME OF ANIMAL ....
WHERE I WANT TO GO TO SEE IT ....
TYPE OF PLACE ....

....
NOTES ....

DATE SEEN ..../......./...........

MY BUCKET LIST OF WILDLIFE TO SEE

NAME OF ANIMAL ....

WHERE I WANT TO GO TO SEE IT ....

TYPE OF PLACE ....

NOTES ....

DATE SEEN ..../......../..........

NAME OF ANIMAL ....

WHERE I WANT TO GO TO SEE IT ....

TYPE OF PLACE ....

NOTES ....

DATE SEEN ..../......../..........

NAME OF ANIMAL ....

WHERE I WANT TO GO TO SEE IT ....

TYPE OF PLACE ....

NOTES ....

DATE SEEN ..../......../..........

MY BUCKET LIST of WILDLIFE TO SEE

NAME OF ANIMAL

WHERE I WANT TO GO TO SEE IT

TYPE OF PLACE

NOTES

DATE SEEN .... / .... / ....

NAME OF ANIMAL

WHERE I WANT TO GO TO SEE IT

TYPE OF PLACE

NOTES

DATE SEEN .... / .... / ....

NAME OF ANIMAL

WHERE I WANT TO GO TO SEE IT

TYPE OF PLACE

NOTES

DATE SEEN .... / .... / ....

MY BUCKET LIST of WILDLIFE TO SEE

NAME OF ANIMAL ....
WHERE I WANT TO GO TO SEE IT ....
TYPE OF PLACE ....
....

NOTES ....

DATE SEEN ..../......./.........

NAME OF ANIMAL ....
WHERE I WANT TO GO TO SEE IT ....
TYPE OF PLACE ....
....

NOTES ....

DATE SEEN ..../......./.........

NAME OF ANIMAL ....
WHERE I WANT TO GO TO SEE IT ....
TYPE OF PLACE ....
....

NOTES ....

DATE SEEN ..../......./.........

MY BUCKET LIST of WILDLIFE TO SEE

NAME OF ANIMAL ....

WHERE I WANT TO GO TO SEE IT ....

TYPE OF PLACE ....

NOTES ....

DATE SEEN ..../......../........

NAME OF ANIMAL ....

WHERE I WANT TO GO TO SEE IT ....

TYPE OF PLACE ....

NOTES ....

DATE SEEN ..../......../........

NAME OF ANIMAL ....

WHERE I WANT TO GO TO SEE IT ....

TYPE OF PLACE ....

NOTES ....

DATE SEEN ..../......../........

NIGHT SKIES
MEET ME UNDER THE STARS

THINGS ARE ALWAYS LOOKING UP in the great outdoors, including the night life.

Our planet is only a speck in the greater outdoors of outer space, with vast views of the cosmos. One of the great joys of being out in the wilderness can be the showcase above, the connective joy of seeing part of our galaxy, the Milky Way, arc deliciously across the sky.

You may want to head to a dark sky preserve, away from the light pollution of humans. Canada offers many, from the beautiful Jasper National Park to Wood Hole National Park, which claims to be the largest dark sky preserve in the world.

Celestial objects are on the move. The earth rotates every 24 hours, orbits the sun every 365 days, and has a moon that orbits it every 28 days. Other spheres in the sky also rotate and orbit, so what you can see in a night sky depends on where you are and what time of year and night it is. Different constellations of stars are seen in the Southern Hemisphere than those visible north of the equator.

Observatories around the globe can help you enjoy even more of the night sky with powerful telescopes. Most offer websites describing what can be seen in the area with the naked eye. For a stellar dose close to home, you may want to hook up with a local astronomy club for sky watch parties.

If you're ready to go cosmic with your bucket list, here are some heavenly phenomena that can keep your nightlife above it all.

MEET ME UNDER THE STARS

NAKED EYE TIME for CELESTIAL BUCKET LIST

Tip: Planning an activity or trip for the night skies is a lesson in trade-offs. The fuller the beautiful moon, the less you will be able to see of the stars.

	ADD TO BUCKET LIST	DATE SEEN	WHERE
Constellations			
Big Dipper, or *Ursa Major*			
Cassiopeia			
Orion			
Constellations of the zodiac			
International Space Station			
Lunar eclipse			
Meteorite showers			
Perseids in late summer			
Leonids in the fall			
Milky Way			
Moons			
Blue (2nd full moon in a month)			
Crescent moon			
Full moon			
Waning gibbous moon			
Waxing gibbous moon			
North Star, or *Polaris*			

	ADD TO BUCKET LIST	DATE SEEN	WHERE
Planets visible with the naked eye			
Jupiter			
Mars			
Neptune			
Saturn			
Venus			
Satellites			
Dog Star, or *Sirius* (the brightest star visible from Earth)			
Solar eclipse			

Write in any additional celestial events you would like to witness.

CELESTIAL NOTES

Use the following pages to record your full-moon hike or your sky watch party or your dreamy thoughts while observing the beautiful night sky.

DATE SEEN _____ / _____ / _____ WHERE _____

DESCRIBE WHAT HAPPENED AND HOW IT LOOKED _____

_____

_____

_____

DATE SEEN _____ / _____ / _____ WHERE _____

DESCRIBE WHAT HAPPENED AND HOW IT LOOKED _____

_____

_____

_____

DATE SEEN _____ / _____ / _____ WHERE _____

DESCRIBE WHAT HAPPENED AND HOW IT LOOKED _____

_____

_____

_____

DATE SEEN _____ / _____ / _____ WHERE _____

DESCRIBE WHAT HAPPENED AND HOW IT LOOKED _____

_____

_____

_____

CELESTIAL NOTES

DATE SEEN _____ / _____ / _____ WHERE _____
DESCRIBE WHAT HAPPENED AND HOW IT LOOKED _____
_____
_____
_____

DATE SEEN _____ / _____ / _____ WHERE _____
DESCRIBE WHAT HAPPENED AND HOW IT LOOKED _____
_____
_____
_____

DATE SEEN _____ / _____ / _____ WHERE _____
DESCRIBE WHAT HAPPENED AND HOW IT LOOKED _____
_____
_____
_____

DATE SEEN _____ / _____ / _____ WHERE _____
DESCRIBE WHAT HAPPENED AND HOW IT LOOKED _____
_____
_____
_____

CELESTIAL NOTES

DATE SEEN ..... / ..... / .... WHERE ....
DESCRIBE WHAT HAPPENED AND HOW IT LOOKED ....
....
....
....

DATE SEEN ..... / ..... / .... WHERE ....
DESCRIBE WHAT HAPPENED AND HOW IT LOOKED ....
....
....
....

DATE SEEN ..... / ..... / .... WHERE ....
DESCRIBE WHAT HAPPENED AND HOW IT LOOKED ....
....
....
....

DATE SEEN ..... / ..... / .... WHERE ....
DESCRIBE WHAT HAPPENED AND HOW IT LOOKED ....
....
....
....

CELESTIAL NOTES

DATE SEEN _____ / _____ / _____ WHERE _____
DESCRIBE WHAT HAPPENED AND HOW IT LOOKED _____
_____
_____
_____

DATE SEEN _____ / _____ / _____ WHERE _____
DESCRIBE WHAT HAPPENED AND HOW IT LOOKED _____
_____
_____
_____

DATE SEEN _____ / _____ / _____ WHERE _____
DESCRIBE WHAT HAPPENED AND HOW IT LOOKED _____
_____
_____
_____

DATE SEEN _____ / _____ / _____ WHERE _____
DESCRIBE WHAT HAPPENED AND HOW IT LOOKED _____
_____
_____
_____

CELESTIAL NOTES

DATE SEEN ..... / ..... / .... WHERE ....
DESCRIBE WHAT HAPPENED AND HOW IT LOOKED ....
....
....
....

DATE SEEN ..... / ..... / .... WHERE ....
DESCRIBE WHAT HAPPENED AND HOW IT LOOKED ....
....
....
....

DATE SEEN ..... / ..... / .... WHERE ....
DESCRIBE WHAT HAPPENED AND HOW IT LOOKED ....
....
....
....

DATE SEEN ..... / ..... / .... WHERE ....
DESCRIBE WHAT HAPPENED AND HOW IT LOOKED ....
....
....
....

CELESTIAL NOTES

DATE SEEN ..../......./........   WHERE ....
DESCRIBE WHAT HAPPENED AND HOW IT LOOKED ....
....
....
....

DATE SEEN ..../......./........   WHERE ....
DESCRIBE WHAT HAPPENED AND HOW IT LOOKED ....
....
....
....

DATE SEEN ..../......./........   WHERE ....
DESCRIBE WHAT HAPPENED AND HOW IT LOOKED ....
....
....
....

DATE SEEN ..../......./........   WHERE ....
DESCRIBE WHAT HAPPENED AND HOW IT LOOKED ....
....
....
....

CELESTIAL NOTES

DATE SEEN ...... / ...... / .... WHERE ....
DESCRIBE WHAT HAPPENED AND HOW IT LOOKED ....
....
....
....

DATE SEEN ...... / ...... / .... WHERE ....
DESCRIBE WHAT HAPPENED AND HOW IT LOOKED ....
....
....
....

DATE SEEN ...... / ...... / .... WHERE ....
DESCRIBE WHAT HAPPENED AND HOW IT LOOKED ....
....
....
....

DATE SEEN ...... / ...... / .... WHERE ....
DESCRIBE WHAT HAPPENED AND HOW IT LOOKED ....
....
....
....

CELESTIAL NOTES

DATE SEEN ..... / ..... / ..... WHERE ....
DESCRIBE WHAT HAPPENED AND HOW IT LOOKED ....
....
....
....

DATE SEEN ..... / ..... / ..... WHERE ....
DESCRIBE WHAT HAPPENED AND HOW IT LOOKED ....
....
....
....

DATE SEEN ..... / ..... / ..... WHERE ....
DESCRIBE WHAT HAPPENED AND HOW IT LOOKED ....
....
....
....

DATE SEEN ..... / ..... / ..... WHERE ....
DESCRIBE WHAT HAPPENED AND HOW IT LOOKED ....
....
....
....

CELESTIAL NOTES

DATE SEEN ____ / ____ / _____ WHERE ....
DESCRIBE WHAT HAPPENED AND HOW IT LOOKED ....
....
....
....

DATE SEEN ____ / ____ / _____ WHERE ....
DESCRIBE WHAT HAPPENED AND HOW IT LOOKED ....
....
....
....

DATE SEEN ____ / ____ / _____ WHERE ....
DESCRIBE WHAT HAPPENED AND HOW IT LOOKED ....
....
....
....

DATE SEEN ____ / ____ / _____ WHERE ....
DESCRIBE WHAT HAPPENED AND HOW IT LOOKED ....
....
....
....

CELESTIAL NOTES

DATE SEEN ...... / ...... / .... WHERE ....
DESCRIBE WHAT HAPPENED AND HOW IT LOOKED ....
....
....
....

DATE SEEN ...... / ...... / .... WHERE ....
DESCRIBE WHAT HAPPENED AND HOW IT LOOKED ....
....
....
....

DATE SEEN ...... / ...... / .... WHERE ....
DESCRIBE WHAT HAPPENED AND HOW IT LOOKED ....
....
....
....

DATE SEEN ...... / ...... / .... WHERE ....
DESCRIBE WHAT HAPPENED AND HOW IT LOOKED ....
....
....
....

CELESTIAL NOTES

DATE SEEN ____ / ____ / _____ WHERE ....
DESCRIBE WHAT HAPPENED AND HOW IT LOOKED ....
....
....
....

DATE SEEN ____ / ____ / _____ WHERE ....
DESCRIBE WHAT HAPPENED AND HOW IT LOOKED ....
....
....
....

DATE SEEN ____ / ____ / _____ WHERE ....
DESCRIBE WHAT HAPPENED AND HOW IT LOOKED ....
....
....
....

DATE SEEN ____ / ____ / _____ WHERE ....
DESCRIBE WHAT HAPPENED AND HOW IT LOOKED ....
....
....
....

CELESTIAL NOTES

DATE SEEN ____/____/____ WHERE _____
DESCRIBE WHAT HAPPENED AND HOW IT LOOKED _____
_____
_____
_____

DATE SEEN ____/____/____ WHERE _____
DESCRIBE WHAT HAPPENED AND HOW IT LOOKED _____
_____
_____
_____

DATE SEEN ____/____/____ WHERE _____
DESCRIBE WHAT HAPPENED AND HOW IT LOOKED _____
_____
_____
_____

DATE SEEN ____/____/____ WHERE _____
DESCRIBE WHAT HAPPENED AND HOW IT LOOKED _____
_____
_____
_____

WORDS ABOUT NATURE

JOURNALING ABOUT NATURE and the great outdoors has an intriguing legacy that may inspire your own freedom of expression.

Transcendentalist David Henry Thoreau (1817-1862), naturalist John Muir (1838-1914), and author Nathaniel Hawthorne (1804-1864) all wrote about the relationships between the nature of humans and Mother Nature.

Read on to find out about Thoreau's felicity of solitude in nature, Muir's observation of both the glories outdoors and the guts of predators and prey, and Hawthorne's musings on which seasons trigger decay and which spark living for "the simple end of being happy."

THINGS TO PACK ON A ADVENTURE

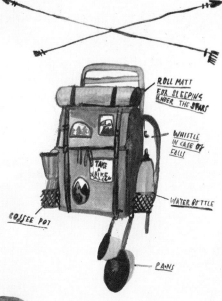

ROLL MATT FOR SLEEPING UNDER THE STARS

WHISTLE IN CASE OF FALLS

WATER BOTTLE

COFFEE POT

PANS

SLEEPING BAGS

 BINOCULARS

 FIRST AID KIT

 SARDINES

 KINDLING

 POCKET KNIFE

 DUCT TAPE

SOLITUDE

BY HENRY DAVID THOREAU

THIS IS A DELICIOUS EVENING, when the whole body is one sense, and imbibes delight through every pore. I go and come with a strange liberty in Nature, a part of herself. As I walk along the stony shore of the pond in my shirt-sleeves, though it is cool as well as cloudy and windy, and I see nothing special to attract me, all the elements are unusually congenial to me. The bullfrogs trump to usher in the night, and the note of the whip-poor-will is borne on the rippling wind from over the water. Sympathy with the fluttering alder and poplar leaves almost takes away my breath; yet, like the lake, my serenity is rippled but not ruffled. These small waves raised by the evening wind are as remote from storm as the smooth reflecting surface. Though it is now dark, the wind still blows and roars in the wood, the waves still dash, and some creatures lull the rest with their notes. The repose is never complete. The wildest animals do not repose, but seek their prey now; the fox, and skunk, and rabbit, now roam the fields and woods without fear. They are Nature's watchmen—links which connect the days of animated life.

When I return to my house I find that visitors have been there and left their cards, either a bunch of flowers, or a wreath of evergreen, or a name in pencil on a yellow walnut leaf or a chip. They who come rarely to the woods take some little piece of the forest into their hands to play with by the way, which they leave, either intentionally or accidentally. One has peeled a willow wand, woven it into a ring, and dropped it on my table. I could always tell if visitors had called in my absence, either by the bended twigs or grass, or the print of their shoes, and generally of what sex or age or quality they were by some slight trace left, as a flower dropped, or a bunch of grass plucked and thrown away, even as far off as the railroad, half a mile distant, or by the lingering odor of a cigar or pipe. Nay, I was frequently notified of the passage of a traveller along the highway sixty rods off by the scent of his pipe.

There is commonly sufficient space about us. Our horizon is never quite at our elbows. The thick wood is not just at our door, nor the pond, but somewhat is always clearing, familiar and worn by us, appropriated and fenced in some way, and reclaimed from Nature. For what reason have I this vast range and circuit, some square miles of unfrequented forest, for my privacy, abandoned to me by men? My nearest neighbor is a mile distant, and no house is visible from any place but the hill-tops within half a mile of my own. I have my horizon bounded by woods all to myself; a distant view of the railroad where it touches the pond on the one hand, and of the fence which skirts the woodland road on the other. But for the most part it is as solitary where I live as on the prairies. It is as much Asia or Africa as New England. I have, as it were, my own sun and moon and stars, and a little world all to myself. At night there was never a traveller passed my house, or knocked at my door, more than if I were the first or last man; unless it were in the spring, when at long intervals some came from the village to fish for pouts— they plainly fished much more in the Walden Pond of their own natures, and baited their hooks with darkness—but they soon retreated, usually with light baskets, and left "the world to darkness and to me," and the black kernel of the night was never profaned by any human neighborhood. I believe that men are generally still a little afraid of the dark, though the witches are all hung, and Christianity and candles have been introduced.

Yet I experienced sometimes that the most sweet and tender, the most innocent and encouraging society may be found in any natural object, even for the poor misanthrope and most melancholy man. There can be no very black melancholy to him who lives in the midst of Nature and has his senses still. There was never yet such a storm but it was Æolian music to a healthy and innocent ear. Nothing can rightly compel a simple and brave man to a vulgar sadness. While I enjoy the friendship of the seasons I trust that nothing can make life a burden to me. The gentle rain which waters my beans and keeps me in the house today is not drear and melancholy, but good for me too. Though it prevents my hoeing them, it is of far more worth than my hoeing. If it should continue so long as to cause the seeds to rot in the ground and destroy the potatoes in the low lands, it would still be good for the grass on the uplands, and, being good for the grass, it would be good for me. Sometimes, when I compare myself with other men, it seems as if I were more favored by the gods than they, beyond any deserts that I am conscious of; as if I had a warrant and surety at their hands which my fellows have not, and were especially guided and guarded. I do not flatter myself, but if it be possible they flatter me. I have never felt lonesome, or in the least oppressed by a sense of solitude, but once, and that was a few weeks after I came to the woods, when, for an hour, I doubted if the near neighborhood of man was not essential to a serene and healthy life. To be alone was something unpleasant. But I was at the same time conscious of a slight insanity in my mood, and seemed to foresee my recovery. In the midst of a gentle rain while these thoughts prevailed, I was suddenly sensible of such sweet and beneficent society in Nature, in the very pattering of the drops, and in every sound and sight around my house, an infinite and unaccountable friendliness all at once like an atmosphere sustaining me, as made the fancied advantages of human neighborhood insignificant, and I have never thought of them since. Every little pine needle expanded and swelled with sympathy and befriended me. I was so distinctly made aware of the presence of something kindred to me, even in scenes which we are accustomed to call wild and dreary, and also that the nearest of blood to me and humanest was not a person nor a villager, that I thought no place could ever be strange to me again. …Some of my pleasantest hours were during the long rain-storms in the spring or fall, which confined me to the house for the afternoon as well as the forenoon, soothed by their ceaseless roar and pelting; when an early twilight ushered in a long evening in which many thoughts had time to take root and unfold themselves. In those driving northeast rains which tried the village houses so, when the maids stood ready with mop and pail in front entries to keep the deluge out, I sat behind my door in my little house, which was all entry, and thoroughly enjoyed its protection. In one heavy thunder-shower the lightning struck a large pitch pine across the pond, making a very conspicuous and perfectly regular spiral groove from top to bottom, an inch or more deep, and four or five inches wide, as you would groove a walking-stick. I passed it again the other day, and was struck with awe on looking up and beholding that mark, now more distinct than ever, where a terrific and resistless bolt came down out of the harmless sky eight years ago. Men frequently say to me, "I should think you would feel lonesome down there, and want to be nearer to folks, rainy and snowy days and nights especially." I am tempted to reply to such—This whole earth which we inhabit is but a point in space. How far apart, think you, dwell the two most distant inhabitants of yonder star, the breadth of whose disk cannot be appreciated by our instruments? Why should I feel lonely? Is not our planet in the Milky Way? This which you put seems to me not to be the most important question. What sort of space is that which separates a man from his fellows and makes him solitary? I have found that no exertion of the legs can bring two minds much nearer to one another. What do we want most to dwell near to? Not to many men surely, the depot, the post-office, the bar-room, the meeting-house, the school-house, the grocery, Beacon Hill, or the Five Points, where men most congregate, but to the perennial source of our life, whence in all our experience we have found that to issue, as the willow stands near the water and sends out its roots in that direction. This will vary with different natures, but this is the place where a wise man will dig his cellar…. I one evening overtook one of my townsmen, who has accumulated what is called "a handsome property"—though I never got a *fair* view of it—on the Walden road, driving a pair of cattle to market, who inquired of me how I could bring my mind to give up so many of the comforts of life. I answered that I was very sure I liked it passably well; I was not joking. And so I went home to my bed, and left him to pick his way through the darkness and the mud to Brighton—or Bright-town—which place he would reach some time in the morning.

Any prospect of awakening or coming to life to a dead man makes indifferent all times and places. The place where that may occur is always the same, and indescribably pleasant to all our senses. For the most part we allow only outlying and transient circumstances to make our occasions. They are, in fact, the cause of our distraction. Nearest to all things is that power which fashions their being. *Next* to us the grandest laws are continually being executed. *Next* to us is not the workman whom we have hired, with whom we love so well to talk, but the workman whose work we are.

The indescribable innocence and beneficence of Nature—of sun and wind and rain, of summer and winter—such health, such cheer, they afford forever! and such sympathy have they ever with our race, that all Nature would be affected, and the sun's brightness fade, and the winds would sigh humanely, and the clouds rain tears, and the woods shed their leaves and put on mourning in midsummer, if any man should ever for a just cause grieve. Shall I not have intelligence with the earth? Am I not partly leaves and vegetable mould myself?

MY FIRST SUMMER IN THE SIERRA

THE MONO TRAIL 🐦 BY JOHN MUIR

AUGUST 13: Day all sunshine, dawn and evening purple, noon gold, no clouds, air motionless. Mr. Delaney arrived with two shepherds, one of them an Indian. On his way up from the plains he left some provisions at the Portuguese camp on Porcupine Creek near our old Yosemite camp, and I set out this morning with one of the pack animals to fetch them. Arrived at the Porcupine camp at noon, and might have returned to the Tuolumne late in the evening, but concluded to stay overnight with the Portuguese shepherds at their pressing invitation. They had sad stories to tell of losses from the Yosemite bears, and were so discouraged they seemed on the point of leaving the mountains; for the bears came every night and helped themselves to one or several of the flock in spite of all their efforts to keep them off.

I spent the afternoon in a grand ramble along the Yosemite walls. From the highest of the rocks called the Three Brothers, I enjoyed a magnificent view comprehending all the upper half of the floor of the valley and nearly all the rocks of the walls on both sides and at the head, with snowy peaks in the background. Saw also the Vernal and Nevada Falls, a truly glorious picture—rocky strength and permanence combined with beauty of plants frail and fine and evanescent; water descending in thunder, and the same water gliding through meadows and groves in gentlest beauty. This standpoint is about eight thousand feet above the sea, or four thousand feet above the floor of the valley, and every tree, though looking small and feathery, stands in admirable clearness, and the shadows they cast are as distinct in outline as if seen at a distance of a few yards. They appeared even more so. No words will ever describe the exquisite beauty and charm of this mountain park—Nature's landscape garden at once tenderly beautiful and sublime. No wonder it draws nature-lovers from all over the world. Glacial action even on this lofty summit is plainly displayed. Not only has all the lovely valley now smiling in sunshine been filled to the brim with ice, but it has been deeply overflowed. I visited our old Yosemite camp-ground on the head of Indian Creek, and found it fairly patted and smoothed down with bear-tracks. The bears had eaten all the sheep that were smothered in the corral, and some of the grand animals must have died, for Mr. Delaney, before leaving camp, put a large quantity of poison in the carcasses. All sheep-men carry strychnine to kill coyotes, bears, and panthers, though neither coyotes nor panthers are at all numerous in the upper mountains. The little dog-like wolves are far more numerous in the foothill region and on the plains, where they find a better supply of food—saw only one panther-track above eight thousand feet. On my return after sunset to the Portuguese camp I found the shepherds greatly excited over the behavior of the bears that have learned to like mutton. "They are getting worse and worse," they lamented. Not willing to wait decently until after dark for their suppers, they come and kill and eat their fill in broad daylight. The evening before my arrival, when the two shepherds were leisurely driving the flock toward camp half an hour before sunset, a hungry bear came out of the chaparral within a few yards of them and shuffled deliberately toward the flock. "Portuguese Joe," who always carried a gun loaded with buckshot, fired excitedly, threw down his gun, fled to the nearest suitable tree, and climbed to a safe height without waiting to see the effect of his shot. His companion also ran, but said that he saw the bear rise on its hind legs and throw out its arms as if feeling for somebody, and then go into the brush as if wounded.

At another of their camps in this neighborhood, a bear with two cubs attacked the flock before sunset, just as they were approaching the corral. Joe promptly climbed a tree out of danger, while Antone, rebuking his companion for cowardice in abandoning his charge, said that he was not going to let bears "eat up his sheeps" in daylight, and rushed towards the bears, shouting and setting his dog on them. The frightened cubs climbed a tree, but the mother ran to meet the shepherd and seemed anxious to fight. Antone stood astonished for a moment, eyeing the oncoming bear, then turned and fled, closely pursued. Unable to reach a suitable tree for climbing, he ran to the camp and scrambled up to the roof of the little cabin; the bear followed, but did not climb to the roof —only stood glaring up at him for a few minutes, threatening him and holding him in mortal terror, then went to her cubs, called them down, went to the flock, caught a sheep for supper, and vanished in the brush. As soon as the bear left the cabin, the trembling Antone begged Joe to show him a good safe tree, up which he climbed like a sailor climbing a mast, and remained as long as he could hold on, the tree being almost branchless. After these disastrous experiences the two shepherds chopped and gathered large piles of dry wood and made a ring of fire around the corral every night, while one with a gun kept watch from a comfortable stage built on a neighboring pine that commanded a view of the corral. This evening the show made by the circle of fire was very fine, bringing out the surrounding trees in most impressive relief, and making the thousands of sheep eyes glow like a glorious bed of diamonds.

AUGUST 14: Up to the time I went to bed last night all was quiet, though we expected the shaggy freebooters every minute. They did not come till near midnight, when a pair walked boldly to the corral between two of the great fires, climbed in, killed two sheep and smothered ten, while the frightened watcher in the tree did not fire a single shot, saying that he was afraid he might kill some of the sheep, for the bears got into the corral before he got a good clear view of them. I told the shepherds they should at once move the flock to another camp. "Oh, no use, no use," they lamented; "where we go, the bears go too. See my poor dead sheeps—soon all dead. No use try another camp. We go down to the plains." And as I afterwards learned, they were driven out of the mountains a month before the usual time. Were bears much more numerous and destructive, the sheep would be kept away altogether.

It seems strange that bears, so fond of all sorts of flesh, running the risks of guns and fires and poison, should never attack men except in defense of their young. How easily and safely a bear could pick us up as we lie asleep! Only wolves and tigers seem to have learned to hunt man for food, and perhaps sharks and crocodiles. Mosquitoes and other insects would, I suppose, devour a helpless man in some parts of the world, and so might lions, leopards, wolves, hyenas, and panthers at times if pressed by hunger,—but under ordinary circumstances, perhaps, only the tiger among land animals may be said to be a man-eater,—unless we add man himself.

Clouds as usual about .05. Another glorious Sierra day, warm, crisp, fragrant, and clear. Many of the flowering plants have gone to seed, but many others are unfolding their petals every day, and the firs and pines are more fragrant than ever. Their seeds are nearly ripe, and will soon be flying in the merriest flocks that ever spread a wing.

BUDS AND BIRD-VOICES

NATHANIEL HAWTHORNE

BALMY SPRING—weeks later than we expected, and months later than we longed for her—comes at last to revive the moss on the roof and walls of our old mansion. She peeps brightly into my study window, inviting me to throw it open and create a summer atmosphere by the intermixture of her genial breath with the black and cheerless comfort of the stove. As the casement ascends, forth into infinite space fly the innumerable forms of thought or fancy that have kept me company in the retirement of this little chamber during the sluggish lapse of wintry weather—visions gay, grotesque and sad, pictures of real life tinted with nature's homely gray and russet, scenes in dreamland bedizened with rainbow-hues which faded before they were well laid on. All these may vanish now, and leave me to mold a fresh existence out of sunshine. Brooding Meditation may flap her dusky wings and take her owl-like flight, blinking amid the cheerfulness of noontide. Such companions befit the season of frosted window-panes and crackling fires, when the blast howls through the black-ash trees of our avenue, and the drifting snowstorm chokes up the wood paths and fills the highway from stone wall to stone wall. In the spring and summer time all somber thoughts should follow the winter northward with the somber and thoughtful crows. The old paradisiacal economy of life is again in force: we live, not to think nor to labor, but for the simple end of being happy; nothing for the present hour is worthy of man's infinite capacity save to imbibe the warm smile of heaven and sympathize with the reviving earth.

The present Spring comes onward with fleeter footsteps because Winter lingered so unconscionably long that with her best diligence she can hardly retrieve half the allotted period of her reign. It is but a fortnight since I stood on the brink of our swollen river and beheld the accumulated ice of four frozen months go down the stream. Except in streaks here and there upon the hillsides, the whole visible universe was then covered with deep snow the nethermost layer of which had been deposited by an early December storm. It was a sight to make the beholder torpid, in the impossibility of imagining how this vast white napkin was to be removed from the face of the corpse-like world in less time than had been required to spread it there. But who can estimate the power of gentle influences, whether amid material desolation or the moral winter of man's heart? There have been no tempestuous rains—even no sultry days—but a constant breath of southern winds, with now a day of kindly sunshine, and now a no less kindly mist, or a soft descent of showers, in which a smile and a blessing seemed to have been steeped. The snow has vanished as if by magic; whatever heaps may be hidden in the woods and deep gorges of the hills, only two solitary specks remain in the landscape, and those I shall almost regret to miss when to-morrow I look for them in vain. Never before, methinks, has spring pressed so closely on the footsteps of retreating winter. Along the roadside the green blades of grass have sprouted on the very edge of the snowdrifts. The pastures and mowing fields have not yet assumed a general aspect of verdure, but neither have they the cheerless brown tint which they wear in later autumn, when vegetation has entirely ceased; there is now a faint shadow of life, gradually brightening into the warm reality. Some tracts in a happy exposure—as, for instance, yonder southwestern slope of an orchard, in front of that old red farmhouse beyond the river—such patches of land already wear a beautiful and tender green to which no future luxuriance can add a charm. It looks unreal—a prophecy, a hope, a transitory effect of some peculiar light, which will vanish with the slightest motion of the eye. But beauty is never a delusion; not these verdant tracts but the dark and barren landscape all around them is a shadow and a dream. Each moment wins some portion of the earth from death to life; a sudden gleam of verdure brightens along the sunny slope of a bank which an instant ago was brown and bare. You look again, and, behold an apparition of green grass!

The trees in our orchard and elsewhere are as yet naked, but already appear full of life and vegetable blood. It seems as if by one magic touch they might instantaneously burst into full foliage, and that the wind which now sighs through their naked branches might make sudden music amid innumerable leaves. The moss-grown willow tree which for forty years past has overshadowed these western windows will be among the first to put on its green attire. There are some objections to the willow: it is not a dry and cleanly tree, and impresses the beholder with an association of sliminess. No trees, I think, are perfectly agreeable as companions unless they have glossy leaves, dry bark, and a firm and hard texture of trunk and branches. But the willow is almost the earliest to gladden us with the promise and reality of beauty in its graceful and delicate foliage, and the last to scatter its yellow, yet scarcely-withered, leaves upon the ground. All through the winter, too, its yellow twigs give it a sunny aspect which is not without a cheering influence even in the grayest and gloomiest day. Beneath a clouded sky it faithfully remembers the sunshine. Our old house would lose a charm were the willow to be cut down, with its golden crown over the snow-covered roof, and its heap of summer verdure.

The lilac shrubs under my study windows are likewise almost in leaf; in two or three days more I may put forth my hand and pluck the topmost bough in its freshest green. These lilacs are very aged, and have lost the luxuriant foliage of their prime. The heart or the judgment or the moral sense or the taste is dissatisfied with their present aspect. Old age is not venerable when it embodies itself in lilacs, rose-bushes, or any other ornamental shrubs; it seems as if such plants, as they grow only for beauty, ought to flourish only in immortal youth—or, at least, to die before their sad decrepitude. Trees of beauty are trees of paradise, and therefore not subject to decay by their original nature, though they have lost that precious birthright by being transplanted to an earthly soil. There is a kind of ludicrous unfitness in the idea of a time-stricken and grandfatherly lilac-bush. The analogy holds good in human life. Persons who can only be graceful and ornamental—who can give the world nothing but flowers—should die young, and never be seen with gray hair and wrinkles, any more than the flower-shrubs with mossy bark and blighted foliage, like the lilacs under my window. Not that beauty is worthy of less than immortality. No; the beautiful should live forever, and thence, perhaps, the sense of impropriety when we see it triumphed over by time. Apple trees, on the other hand, grow old without reproach. Let them live as long as they may, and contort themselves into whatever perversity of shape they please, and deck their withered limbs with a springtime gaudiness of pink-blossoms, still they are respectable, even if they afford us only an apple or two in a season. Those few apples—or, at all events, the remembrance of apples in bygone years—are the atonement which utilitarianism inexorably demands for the privilege of lengthened life. Human flower shrubs, if they will grow old on earth, should, besides their lovely blossoms, bear some kind of fruit that will satisfy earthly appetites, else neither man nor the decorum of nature will deem it fit that the moss should gather on them.

One of the first things that strikes the attention when the white sheet of winter is withdrawn is the neglect and disarray that lay hidden beneath it. Nature is not cleanly, according to our prejudices. The beauty of preceding years, now transformed to brown and blighted deformity, obstructs the brightening loveliness of the present hour. Our avenue is strewn with the whole crop of autumn's withered leaves. There are quantities of decayed branches which one tempest after another has flung down, black and rotten, and one or two with the ruin of a bird's nest clinging to them. In the garden are the dried bean-vines, the brown stalks of the asparagus-bed, and melancholy old cabbages which were frozen into the soil before their unthrifty cultivator could find time to gather them. How invariable throughout all the forms of life do we find these intermingled memorials of death! On the soil of thought and in the garden of the heart, as well as in the sensual world, lie withered leaves—the ideas and feelings that we have done with. There is no wind strong enough to sweep them away; infinite space will not garner them from our sight. What mean they? Why may we not be permitted to live and enjoy as if this were the first life and our own the primal enjoyment, instead of treading always on these dry bones and mouldering relics from the aged accumulation of which springs all that now appears so young and new? Sweet must have been the spring-time of Eden, when no earlier year had strewn its decay upon the virgin turf, and no former experience had ripened into summer and faded into autumn in the hearts of its inhabitants! That was a world worth living in.—Oh, thou murmurer, it is out of the very wantonness of such a life that thou feignest these idle lamentations. There is no decay. Each human soul is the first created inhabitant of its own Eden.—We dwell in an old moss-covered mansion and tread in the worn footprints of the past and have a gray clergyman's ghost for our daily and nightly inmate, yet all these outward circumstances are made less than visionary by the renewing power of the spirit. Should the spirit ever lose this power—should the withered leaves and the rotten branches and the moss-covered house and the ghost of the gray past ever become its realities, and the verdure and the freshness merely its faint dream—then let it pray to be released from earth. It will need the air of heaven to revive its pristine energies.

NATIONAL PARKS

MORE THAN 6,000 NATIONAL PARKS in more than 100 countries around the world showcase the great outdoors. The concept started in the United States back in 1872 when the U.S. Congress established the Yellowstone National Park, still a favorite for many. Writer Wallace Stegner called national parks "the best idea we ever had." What are your ideas to enjoy the splendors?

PATAGONIA

NATIONAL PARKS IN THE UNITED STATES

Parks listed in **bold** are among the top ten most visited National Parks in the United States, hosting over two and a half million annually.

DATE VISITED	ADD TO BUCKET LIST	
		Denali, Alaska
		Gates of the Arctic, Alaska
		Glacier Bay, Alaska
		Katmai, Alaska
		Kenai Fjords, Alaska
		Kobuk Valley, Alaska
		Lake Clark, Alaska
		Wrangell-St. Elias, Alaska
		American Samoa, American Samoa
		Grand Canyon, Arizona
		Petrified Forest, Arizona
		Saguaro, Arizona
		Hot Springs, Arkansas
		Channel Islands, California
		Death Valley, California-Nevada
		Joshua Tree, California
		Kings Canyon, California
		Lassen Volcanic, California
		Pinnacles, California

Redwood, California

Sequoia, California

Yosemite, California

Black Canyon of the Gunnison, Colorado

Great Sand Dunes, Colorado

Mesa Verde, Colorado

Rocky Mountain, Colorado

Biscayne, Florida

Dry Tortugas, Florida

Everglades, Florida

Haleakala, Hawaii

Hawai'i Volcanoes, Hawaii

Mammoth Cave, Kentucky

Acadia, Maine

Isle Royale, Michigan

Voyageurs, Minnesota

Glacier, Montana

Great Basin, Nevada

Carlsbad Caverns, New Mexico

Theodore Roosevelt, North Dakota

Crater Lake, Oregon

Cuyahoga Valley, Ohio

Congaree, South Carolina

Badlands, South Dakota

Wind Cave, South Dakota

Great Smoky Mountains, Tennessee-North Carolina

As if 59 National Parks didn't provide enough choices for bucket lists, the U.S. National Park Service also oversees many National Preserves, National Seashores, National Rivers, and National Monuments—from the smallest at .02 acres (Thaddeus Kosciuszko National Memorial in Pennsylvania), to the largest of 13.2 million acres (Wrangell-St. Elias National Park and Preserve in Alaska). National Park Service sites enjoy more than 290 million visits a year! Where do you want to explore?

TOP TEN MOST VISITED PLACES IN THE NATIONAL PARK SYSTEM

BEEN
THERE

ADD TO
BUCKET LIST

#1 Golden Gate National Recreation Area

#2 Blue Ridge Parkway

#3 Great Smoky Mountains National Park

#4 George Washington Memorial Parkway

#5 Lincoln Memorial

#6 Lake Mead National Recreation Area

#7 Gateway National Recreation Area

#8 Natchez Trace Parkway

#9 Chesapeake & Ohio Canal National Historical Park

#10 Grand Canyon National Park

All information in this section was supplied by the National Park System of the United States.

NATIONAL PARKS IN CANADA

You can think big with the Canadian National Parks. They range from the Fundy National Park, which has the world's highest tides, to the Wood Buffalo National Park, which is larger than Switzerland and is a UNESCO World Heritage Site. Thanks to Park Canada for sharing their buzz on their parks in their own words below. You can put a heart next to those you love and a star by those you wish to visit.

Aulavik National Park of Canada
Over 12,000 square kilometers of arctic wilderness on Banks Island.

Auyuittuq National Park of Canada
Baffin Island landscapes containing northern extremity of Canadian Shield.

Banff National Park of Canada
UNESCO World Heritage Site and Canada's first National Park of Canada (est. 1885).

Bruce Peninsula National Park of Canada
Landscapes including the northern end of Niagara Escarpment.

Cape Breton Highlands National Park of Canada
Home to Cabot Trail, a land blessed with spectacular cliffs.

Elk Island National Park of Canada
Alberta plains oasis for rare and endangered species.

Forillon National Park of Canada
The "Jewel of the Gaspé" where land meets sea.

Fundy National Park of Canada
Atlantic's sanctuary with the world's highest tides.

Georgian Bay Islands National Park of Canada
Captivating islands representing Lake Huron's landscape.

Glacier National Park of Canada
British Columbia's lush interior rainforest and permanent glaciers.

Grasslands National Park of Canada
Saskatchewan's rare prairie grasses, dinosaur fossils, and badlands.

Gros Morne National Park of Canada
UNESCO World Heritage Site amid Newfoundland's wild
natural beauty.

Gulf Islands National Park Reserve of Canada
An exceptional coastal island landscape in the southern Strait of Georgia.

Gwaii Haanas National Park Reserve, National Marine Conservation Area
Reserve, and Haida Heritage Site
Haïda culture and coastal rainforest on Queen Charlotte Islands.

Ivvavik National Park of Canada
Calving ground for the Porcupine caribou herd.

Jasper National Park of Canada
UNESCO World Heritage Site and glacial jewel of the Rockies.

Kejimkujik National Park of Canada
Nova Scotia's inland of historic canoe routes and portages.

Kluane National Park and Reserve of Canada
Yukon's UNESCO World Heritage Site contains Canada's highest peak.

Kootenay National Park of Canada
UNESCO World Heritage Site featuring the famous Radium Hot Springs.

Kouchibouguac National Park of Canada
Intricate Acadian blend of coastal and inland habitats.

La Mauricie National Park of Canada
Lakes winding through forested hills for canoe and portage activities.

NATIONAL PARKS IN CANADA

Akami–uapishku-KakKasuak-Mealy Mountains National Park Reserve of Canada
Stunning boreal forest, lakes and rivers protected in the largest federal national park in eastern North America.

Mingan Archipelago National Park Reserve of Canada
A string of islands carved out by the sea.

Mount Revelstoke National Park of Canada
Rainforest of 1,000-year-old cedars and spectacular mountains.

Nááts'ihch'oh National Park Reserve
Measuring 4,850 square kilometers, Nááts'ihch'oh National Park Reserve adjoins Nahanni National Park Reserve and it touches the Yukon boundary to the West.

Nahanni National Park Reserve of Canada
Northwest Territories' UNESCO World Heritage Site.

Pacific Rim National Park Reserve of Canada
Pacific Coast Mountains make up this marine and forest environment.

Point Pelee National Park of Canada
Most southern point on Canadian mainland.

Prince Albert National Park of Canada
Protects slice of northern coniferous forest and wildlife.

Prince Edward Island National Park of Canada
A protected area with spectacular coast.

Qausuittuq National Park of Canada
Over 11,000 square kilometers of wilderness and wildlife to experience in Canada's western high Arctic.

Quttinirpaaq National Park of Canada
Most remote, fragile, rugged, and northerly lands in North America.

Riding Mountain National Park of Canada
Protected island area in the Manitoba Escarpment.

NATIONAL PARKS IN CANADA

Sable Island National Park Reserve of Canada
A wild and windswept island of sand sits far out in the North Atlantic, its iconic crescent shape emerging from the expanse of the sea. Isolated and remote, Sable Island is one of Canada's furthest offshore islands.

Sirmilik National Park of Canada
Northern Baffin Island landscape containing Eastern Arctic Lowlands and Lancaster Sound.

Terra Nova National Park of Canada
Remnants of the Eastern Newfoundland Ancient Appalachian Mountains.

Thousand Islands National Park of Canada
Established in 1904.

Torngat Mountains National Park of Canada
The spectacular wilderness of this National Park comprises 9,700 square kilometers of the Northern Labrador Mountains natural region.

Tuktut Nogait National Park of Canada
Calving ground for the Bluenose caribou herd.

Ukkusiksalik National Park of Canada
The place where there is stone that can be used to carve pots and oil lamps.

Vuntut National Park of Canada
Northern Yukon's unique non-glaciated landscape.

Wapusk National Park of Canada
One of the largest polar bear denning areas in the world.

Waterton Lakes National Park of Canada
International Peace Park; where the Rocky Mountains meet the prairie.

Wood Buffalo National Park of Canada
UNESCO World Heritage Site larger than Switzerland.

Yoho National Park of Canada
UNESCO World Heritage Site in the Rockies.

GREAT BRITAIN'S NATIONAL PARKS

You can put a heart next to those you love and a star by those you wish to visit.

♥ ENGLAND
Ten National Parks cover 9.3% of the country's land area.

The Broads National Park, Norfolk, England
The Broads National Park is home to a network of mostly navigable rivers and lakes in the English counties of Norfolk and Suffolk.

Dartmoor National Park, Devon, England
Dartmoor is an area of moorland in southern Devon, England. The highest point is High Willhays, 621 m (2,037 ft) above sea level. The entire area is rich in antiquities and archaeology.

Exmoor National Park , South West, England
Exmoor National Park is an area of hilly open moorland in west Somerset and north Devon in South West England.

The Lake District, North West England
The Lake District, North West England also known as The Lakes or Lakeland, is a mountainous region in North West England. A popular holiday destination, it is famous for its lakes, forests and mountains and its associations with the early 19th century writings of William Wordsworth and the other Lake Poets.

New Forest National Park, Southeast England
The New Forest is an area of southern England which includes one of the largest remaining tracts of unenclosed pasture land, heathland and forest in the heavily populated south east of England.

Northumberland National Park, Northern England
Northumberland National Park is the northernmost national park in England. It is one of the least populated and least visited of the National Parks. The southernmost part of the park covers the dramatic central section of Hadrian's Wall, dating from the Roman occupation.

North York Moors National Park, North Yorkshire, England
North York Moors National Park containing one of the largest expanses of heather moorland in the United Kingdom.

Peak District National Park, Derbyshire, England
The Peak District is an upland area in England, most of which lies in northern Derbyshire but also includes parts of Cheshire, Greater Manchester, Staffordshire and Yorkshire. The Peak District National Park became the first national park in the United Kingdom in 1951.

South Downs National Park, Southern England
England's newest National Park, having become fully operational on 1 April 2011. The South Downs Way spans the entire length of the park and is the only National Trail that lies wholly within a national park.

Yorkshire Dales National Park, Yorkshire, England
The Yorkshire Dales National Park is crossed by several long-distance routes including the Pennine Way, the Dales Way, the Coast to Coast Walk and the Pennine Bridleway

WALES
Three National Parks cover 19.9% of the country's land area.

Breton Beacons National Park, Wales
The Brecon Beacons National Park is centered on the Brecon Beacons range of hills in southern Wales.

Pembrokeshire Coast National Park, Wales
Pembrokeshire Coast National Park is located along the Pembrokeshire coast in west Wales. It was established as a National Park in 1952, and is the only one in the United Kingdom to have been designated primarily because of its spectacular coastline.

Snowdonia National Park, Wales
Unlike national parks in other countries, Snowdonia (and other such parks in Britain) are made up of both public and private lands under central planning authority.

Two National Parks cover 7.2% of the country's land area.

The Cairngorms National Park, Scotland
> *The Cairngorms National Park is located in north east Scotland,*
> *established in 2003. The park covers the Cairngorms range of mountains,*
> *and surrounding hills. Already the largest national park in the British*
> *Isles, in 2010 it expanded into Highland and Perth and Kinross.*

AUSTRALIA'S NATIONAL PARKS

Australia has hundreds of National Parks with diverse attractions. Some parks highlight cool remnants of the past, like the Australian Fossil Mammal Sites in North Queensland, which UNESCO calls one of the world's Ten great fossil sites. Wollemi Pine Park is home to living trees from a species that flourished when dinosaurs roamed the earth. You can put a heart next to those you love and a star by those you wish to visit.

Bay of Fires Conservation Park
> *Empty beaches with large lichen-covered granite boulders, coastal lagoons*
> *and heathlands covered in wildflowers are the big attractions of both the*
> *Bay of Fires Conservation Park. Until the rest of the world finds out about*
> *the Bay of Fires it's the ultimate place to really get away from it all.*

Carvavon Gorge
> *Carnarvon Gorge is a steep-sided canyon of towering white sandstone*
> *cliffs with lush side gorges full of hanging gardens of mosses and ferns*
> *and sinuously curved ravines with walls so close you can reach out and*
> *touch both sides at once.*

Cradle Mountain Lake St. Clair National Park
> *This park has enough trails to keep you going for days. The Overland*
> *Track takes six days to complete, and really is one of the best long*
> *distance walks in the world.*

Flinders Chase National Park

Known for its amazing wildlife Flinders Chase National Park is home to penguins, fur seals, Australian sea lions, koalas, kangaroos, wallabies plus 254 species of birdlife.

Kakadu National Park

A wonderful place to discover indigenous art sites. Here you'll see an array of rock art covering the walls of ancient gathering places.

Kwiambal National Park

On the junction of the Macintyre and Severn rivers in north-western NSW, Kwiambal National Park has some of the best swimming holes and river gorge scenery you'll see east of the Kimberley, without the tour buses.

Litchfield National Park

In just one relatively small area you can find wetlands and lily-covered billabongs, thundering waterfalls, prolific birdlife and gigantic termite mounds – and the good news is it's only an hour or so drive from Darwin.

Mt. Kosciusko National Park

If you want to climb a mountain you may as well make it Australia's biggest one. Getting to the summit of Mt Kosciuszko National Park is actually a doable, more like a boardwalk stroll, especially if you take the chairlift up the steep bit from Thredbo village, but there are plenty of other lung-busting, thigh-melting mountains and hills to scale in Mt Kosciuszko National Park if you really want to set yourself a challenge.

Nambung National Park

Nambung National Park offer you a spectacular view of thousands of huge surreal looking limestone pillars that rise out of a stark landscape of yellow sand.

Washpool National Park

Washpool National Park is the best spot to get lost in the forest has some wonderful wilderness walks through mossy Tolkienesque forest that will make you feel like you have been teleported into Lord of the Rings. It can be cold and damp in winter, but in summer there's no better place to be.

MY BUCKET LIST FOR NATIONAL PARKS

WHEN ....

DESCRIPTION OF MY EXPERIENCE ....

....

....

....

....

DATE COMPLETED .... / .... / ....

WHEN ....

DESCRIPTION OF MY EXPERIENCE ....

....

....

....

....

DATE COMPLETED .... / .... / ....

WHEN ....

DESCRIPTION OF MY EXPERIENCE ....

....

....

....

....

DATE COMPLETED .... / .... / ....

MY BUCKET LIST for NATIONAL PARKS

WHEN ....

DESCRIPTION OF MY EXPERIENCE ....

....

....

....

....

DATE COMPLETED .... / .... / ....

WHEN ....

DESCRIPTION OF MY EXPERIENCE ....

....

....

....

....

DATE COMPLETED .... / .... / ....

WHEN ....

DESCRIPTION OF MY EXPERIENCE ....

....

....

....

....

DATE COMPLETED .... / .... / ....

MY BUCKET LIST FOR NATIONAL PARKS

WHEN ....

DESCRIPTION OF MY EXPERIENCE ....

....

....

....

....

DATE COMPLETED ..../....../.........

WHEN ....

DESCRIPTION OF MY EXPERIENCE ....

....

....

....

....

DATE COMPLETED ..../....../.........

WHEN ....

DESCRIPTION OF MY EXPERIENCE ....

....

....

....

....

DATE COMPLETED ..../....../.........

MY BUCKET LIST for NATIONAL PARKS

WHEN ....

DESCRIPTION OF MY EXPERIENCE ....

....

....

....

....

DATE COMPLETED .... / .... / ....

WHEN ....

DESCRIPTION OF MY EXPERIENCE ....

....

....

....

....

DATE COMPLETED .... / .... / ....

WHEN ....

DESCRIPTION OF MY EXPERIENCE ....

....

....

....

....

DATE COMPLETED .... / .... / ....

MY BUCKET LIST FOR NATIONAL PARKS

WHEN ....
DESCRIPTION OF MY EXPERIENCE ....
....
....
....
....

DATE COMPLETED .... / .... / ....

WHEN ....
DESCRIPTION OF MY EXPERIENCE ....
....
....
....
....

DATE COMPLETED .... / .... / ....

WHEN ....
DESCRIPTION OF MY EXPERIENCE ....
....
....
....
....

DATE COMPLETED .... / .... / ....

MY BUCKET LIST FOR NATIONAL PARKS

WHEN ....

DESCRIPTION OF MY EXPERIENCE ....

....

....

....

....

DATE COMPLETED .... / .... / ....

WHEN ....

DESCRIPTION OF MY EXPERIENCE ....

....

....

....

....

DATE COMPLETED .... / .... / ....

WHEN ....

DESCRIPTION OF MY EXPERIENCE ....

....

....

....

....

DATE COMPLETED .... / .... / ....

BOTANICAL GARDENS

ARE YOU AN F&F (flora and fauna) kind of person? In addition to compelling animals, do you want to seek out amazing trees and plants? Do you yearn to see the giant lily pads of the Amazon? Walk over the root system and between the 10,000 connected trunks of the Pando in Utah, considered to be one organism—a clonal colony? Do you pine to photograph the bristle pines, believed to be the oldest trees on the planet?

Do the blue poppies of the Himalayas excite you? Are you trying to see more kinds of wildflowers than anyone you know? Do you want to feel dwarfed by the saguaro cactus of the desert? Are you interested in the medicinal uses of plants? Maybe you don't have time to get to the remote outdoors and track down fauna, but you want an urban escape, a flower immersion.

Since the Hanging Gardens of Babylon, regarded as one of the original Seven Wonders of the Ancient World, humans have been gathering the wonders of the wilds to enjoy and study. The Italians started scientific and apothecary gardens in the Renaissance and the Orto Botanico di Padova still exists. These days, many large cities have their own botanical gardens, with plant and tree species from all over the world.

You may not be able to get to all the plants and trees that you want to see in far-flung places, but maybe they can *get to you* in a botanical garden.

Below are some seeds for thought (so to grow) so you can mulch over them. You can create a memorable gardens destination list or noodle opportunities for a special outdoors fix on a more urban trip.

	BEEN THERE	DATE	ADD TO BUCKET LIST
AUSTRALIA			
Royal Botanic Gardens, Sydney			
CANADA			
Jardin Botanique de Montreal			
Montreal Botanic Gardens			
Butchart Gardens, British Columbia			
VanDusen Botanical Garden, British Columbia			
ENGLAND			
Royal Botanical Gardens at Kew			
GERMANY			
Botanischer Garten, Munich			
UNITED STATES			
Desert Botanical Garden, Phoenix, Arizona			
Huntington Botanical Gardens, San Marino, California			
San Francisco Botanical Garden, California			

UNITED STATES (CONTINUED)	BEEN THERE	DATE	ADD TO BUCKET LIST
Denver Botanic Gardens, Colorado			
Fairchild Tropical Botanic Garden, Florida			
Atlanta Botanical Garden, Georgia			
Missouri Botanical Gardens			
Botanic Garden, ABQ Bio Park, Albuquerque, New Mexico			
Brooklyn Botanic Garden, New York			
New York Botanical Gardens, New York			
Franklin Park Conservatory and Botanical Gardens Columbus, Ohio			
Chanticleer Garden, Pennslvania			
Longwood Gardens, Pennsylvania			

These are just some of the botanic gardens worth visiting in a few countries. You can pick a country or continent and go to the website of the Botanic Gardens Conservation International (BGCI) that profiles over 3,000 botanical gardens worldwide. Enter a country name and discover what delights might be down a garden path.

DEADLY & DANGEROUS

BLACK WIDOW

BROWN RECLUSE SPIDER

HOBO SPIDER

TOXIC WITH PAINFUL BITE

BLACK HOUSE SPIDER (FEMALE)

WOLF SPIDER

MOUSE SPIDER

LOW RISK

TRAP DOOR SPIDER

GARDEN ORB WEAVING SPIDER

ST ANDREWS CROSS SPIDER

MY BUCKET LIST FOR BOTANICAL GARDENS

WHERE ....

DESCRIPTION OF MY EXPERIENCE ....

....

....

....

....

DATE COMPLETED ..../......./..........

WHERE ....

DESCRIPTION OF MY EXPERIENCE ....

....

....

....

....

DATE COMPLETED ..../......./..........

WHERE ....

DESCRIPTION OF MY EXPERIENCE ....

....

....

....

....

DATE COMPLETED ..../......./..........

MY BUCKET LIST for BOTANICAL GARDENS

WHERE ....
DESCRIPTION OF MY EXPERIENCE ....
....
....
....
....
....

DATE COMPLETED .... / .... / ....

WHERE ....
DESCRIPTION OF MY EXPERIENCE ....
....
....
....
....

DATE COMPLETED .... / .... / ....

WHERE ....
DESCRIPTION OF MY EXPERIENCE ....
....
....
....
....

DATE COMPLETED .... / .... / ....

MY BUCKET LIST for BOTANICAL GARDENS

WHERE ....

DESCRIPTION OF MY EXPERIENCE ....

....

....

....

....

DATE COMPLETED ..../........./.........

WHERE ....

DESCRIPTION OF MY EXPERIENCE ....

....

....

....

....

DATE COMPLETED ..../........./.........

WHERE ....

DESCRIPTION OF MY EXPERIENCE ....

....

....

....

....

DATE COMPLETED ..../........./.........

MY BUCKET LIST *for* BOTANICAL GARDENS

WHERE ....
DESCRIPTION OF MY EXPERIENCE ....

....

....

....

....

DATE COMPLETED ..../......./.........

WHERE ....
DESCRIPTION OF MY EXPERIENCE ....

....

....

....

....

DATE COMPLETED ..../......./.........

WHERE ....
DESCRIPTION OF MY EXPERIENCE ....

....

....

....

....

DATE COMPLETED ..../......./.........

BIRDS

WHETHER YOU ARE NEW to the joys of setting your sights soaring or are a seasoned pro with feathered friends, the following lists of birding hot spots can inspire some great times in the outdoors. All are beautiful places worth visiting, even if you aren't a birder.

NORTH AMERICAN ROBIN

BALD EAGLE

Stellers Jay

GREAT HORNED OWL

winter wren

AMERICAN KESTREL

BIRD WATCHING

You may want to circle the ones you have been to and put a star next to the ones you want to add to your bucket list of travel wishes.

THE BEST BIRDING SPOTS IN NORTH AMERICA*

ALASKA

The Aleutians & Pribilof Islands
Unlike anything else in North America with ultra-rare Asian vagrants.

ALBERTA

Jasper National Park
A summertime heaven with spectacular scenery and 250 bird species.

ARIZONA

Southeastern Arizona
Desert, canyons and sky islands offer a chance to see Mexican vagrants and desert natives.

CALIFORNIA

Monterey Bay
Pelagic bird (and whale) tours offer up a rich bounty of birds that cannot be seen from land.

Point Reyes National Seashore
Some of the most beautiful scenery on the continent, and a shot at 470 different birds.

The Salton Sea
A vast saline lake in the middle of a desert is like a magnet for birds.

COLORADO

Pawnee National Grasslands
Rare longspurs and sparrows are joined by burrowing owls and ferruginous hawks in these vast open spaces.

DELAWARE

Bombay Hook National Wildlife Refuge
Expansive tidal salt marsh teeming with shorebirds, along with a few rails and bitterns.

FLORIDA
Corkscrew Swamp Sanctuary
Magical boardwalks meander through cypress forests and alligator ponds.

FLORIDA
Ding Darling National Wildlife Refuge
*Vast expanses of wading birds, Roseate Spoonbills and a dozen species
of herons, egrets, and ibises, with Pileated Woodpeckers flying between
the Bald Cypresses.*

HAWAII
Hawaii
*Kauai or the Big Island for the most diversity, or the small, outer islands
for pelagics and rarities, Hawaii is always a treat.*

KANSAS
Cheyenne Bottoms Wildlife Area
*Rails, cranes, shorebirds and 300 other species in the middle of the
Kansas plains.*

MANITOBA
Churchill
A relatively southern spot to view a host of very northern species.

MAINE
Acadia National Park
Gorgeous coastline with a wealth of both ocean and forest birds.

MINNESOTA
Duluth & Sax-Zim Bog
*The frigid winters bring great gray and snowy owls, bohemian waxwings,
and other boreal species.*

NEBRASKA
Platte River
*Every spring, this area hosts the largest concentration of cranes anywhere
in the world.*

NEW JERSEY
Brigantine National Wildlife Refuge
Atlantic City casinos on the horizon, a thousand shorebirds in the foreground.

Cape May
The mecca of Mid-Atlantic birding, with a spring parade of warblers and an autumnal show of hawks.

NEW MEXICO

Bosque del Apache National Wildlife Refuge
Waterfowl, cranes, and eagles mix with roadrunners and quail along the Rio Grande.

NEW YORK

Central Park
Surprisingly, one of the easiest places anywhere to see warblers and other migrants up close.

NORTH CAROLINA

Outer Banks
Marshes meet the sea in these easternmost barrier islands. Great for pelagic tours, too.

NORTH DAKOTA

Potholes & Prairies
Prairie pothole terrain comprised of hundreds of small ponds and marshes, and swarms of birds.

OHIO

Lake Erie Shoreline
Margee Marsh and the surrounding area offer up most of the Eastern birds during migration.

PENNSYLVANIA

Hawk Mountain
Tens of thousands of raptors soar past this premier Eastern hawk-watching spot.

TEXAS

High Island
The first stopover for birds crossing the Gulf of Mexico. A good spring morning can produce a 'fallout' of mythic proportions.

Rio Grande Valley
The holy grail for birders: parrots, green jays, and aplomado falcons are only a few of the wanderers from Mexico.

GREAT BIRDING SPOTS IN AUSTRALIA & EUROPE

AUSTRALIA: Kangaroo Island, Bruny Island, Capertee Valley, Daintree Rainforest, and Atherton Tablelands

BULGARIA: Via Pontica Flyway

ENGLAND: WWT London Wetland Centre, Clay next the Sea

FRANCE: Camargue

HUNGARY: Hortobágy National Park

ICELAND: Jökulsárgljúfur National Park

ITALY: Po Delta

NETHERLANDS & DENMARK: Wadden Sea

NORWAY: Spitsbergen & Svalbard

POLAND & BELARUS: Białowieża Forest

PORTUGAL: Algarve

ROMANIA & UKRAINE: Danube Delta

SPAIN: Doñana National Park, Tarifa

SWEDEN: Falsterbo

These bucket list birding spots in North America, Europe, and Australia are thanks to Jeffrey Kimball—birder, filmmaker, and director of HBO's wonderful Birders: The Central Park Effect.

BIRDS ON MY NATURE BUCKET LIST

BIRD ....
WHERE ....
DESCRIPTION OF MY EXPERIENCE ....
....
....
....

DATE SEEN ...... / ...... / ....

BIRD ....
WHERE ....
DESCRIPTION OF MY EXPERIENCE ....
....
....
....

DATE SEEN ...... / ...... / ....

BIRD ....
WHERE ....
DESCRIPTION OF MY EXPERIENCE ....
....
....
....

DATE SEEN ...... / ...... / ....

BIRDS ON MY NATURE BUCKET LIST

BIRD ....

WHERE ....

DESCRIPTION OF MY EXPERIENCE ....

....

....

....

DATE SEEN ..../......./..........

BIRD ....

WHERE ....

DESCRIPTION OF MY EXPERIENCE ....

....

....

....

DATE SEEN ..../......./..........

BIRD ....

WHERE ....

DESCRIPTION OF MY EXPERIENCE ....

....

....

....

DATE SEEN ..../......./..........

BIRDS ON MY NATURE BUCKET LIST

BIRD
WHERE
DESCRIPTION OF MY EXPERIENCE

DATE SEEN _____ / _____ / _____

BIRD
WHERE
DESCRIPTION OF MY EXPERIENCE

DATE SEEN _____ / _____ / _____

BIRD
WHERE
DESCRIPTION OF MY EXPERIENCE

DATE SEEN _____ / _____ / _____

BIRDS ON MY NATURE BUCKET LIST

BIRD ....

WHERE ....

DESCRIPTION OF MY EXPERIENCE ....

....

....

DATE SEEN ..../......./..........

BIRD ....

WHERE ....

DESCRIPTION OF MY EXPERIENCE ....

....

....

DATE SEEN ..../......./..........

BIRD ....

WHERE ....

DESCRIPTION OF MY EXPERIENCE ....

....

....

DATE SEEN ..../......./..........

BIRDS ON MY NATURE BUCKET LIST

BIRD ....

WHERE ....

DESCRIPTION OF MY EXPERIENCE ....

....

....

....

DATE SEEN ..../......./.........

BIRD ....

WHERE ....

DESCRIPTION OF MY EXPERIENCE ....

....

....

....

DATE SEEN ..../......./.........

BIRD ....

WHERE ....

DESCRIPTION OF MY EXPERIENCE ....

....

....

....

DATE SEEN ..../......./.........

BIRDS ON MY NATURE BUCKET LIST

BIRD ....

WHERE ....

DESCRIPTION OF MY EXPERIENCE ....

....

....

DATE SEEN ..../......./..........

BIRD ....

WHERE ....

DESCRIPTION OF MY EXPERIENCE ....

....

....

DATE SEEN ..../......./..........

BIRD ....

WHERE ....

DESCRIPTION OF MY EXPERIENCE ....

....

....

DATE SEEN ..../......./..........

BIRDS ON MY NATURE BUCKET LIST

BIRD ....
WHERE ....
DESCRIPTION OF MY EXPERIENCE ....

....

....

DATE SEEN .... / .... / ....

BIRD ....
WHERE ....
DESCRIPTION OF MY EXPERIENCE ....

....

....

DATE SEEN .... / .... / ....

BIRD ....
WHERE ....
DESCRIPTION OF MY EXPERIENCE ....

....

....

DATE SEEN .... / .... / ....

BIRDS ON MY NATURE BUCKET LIST

BIRD ....
WHERE ....
DESCRIPTION OF MY EXPERIENCE ....

....

....

....

DATE SEEN ..../......../.........

BIRD ....
WHERE ....
DESCRIPTION OF MY EXPERIENCE ....

....

....

....

DATE SEEN ..../......../.........

BIRD ....
WHERE ....
DESCRIPTION OF MY EXPERIENCE ....

....

....

....

DATE SEEN ..../......../.........

BIRDS ON MY NATURE BUCKET LIST

BIRD ....

WHERE ....

DESCRIPTION OF MY EXPERIENCE ....

....

....

....

DATE SEEN .... / .... / ....

BIRD ....

WHERE ....

DESCRIPTION OF MY EXPERIENCE ....

....

....

....

DATE SEEN .... / .... / ....

BIRD ....

WHERE ....

DESCRIPTION OF MY EXPERIENCE ....

....

....

....

DATE SEEN .... / .... / ....

BIRDS ON NATURE BUCKET LIST

BIRD ....
WHERE ....
DESCRIPTION OF MY EXPERIENCE ....

....

....

DATE SEEN ...... / ...... / ....

BIRD ....
WHERE ....
DESCRIPTION OF MY EXPERIENCE ....

....

....

DATE SEEN ...... / ...... / ....

BIRD ....
WHERE ....
DESCRIPTION OF MY EXPERIENCE ....

....

....

DATE SEEN ...... / ...... / ....

BIRDS ON MY NATURE BUCKET LIST

BIRD ....

WHERE ....

DESCRIPTION OF MY EXPERIENCE ....

....

....

....

DATE SEEN .... / .... / ....

BIRD ....

WHERE ....

DESCRIPTION OF MY EXPERIENCE ....

....

....

....

DATE SEEN .... / .... / ....

BIRD ....

WHERE ....

DESCRIPTION OF MY EXPERIENCE ....

....

....

....

DATE SEEN .... / .... / ....

BIRDS ON MY NATURE BUCKET LIST

BIRD ....
WHERE ....
DESCRIPTION OF MY EXPERIENCE ....
....
....
DATE SEEN ..../........./.........

BIRD ....
WHERE ....
DESCRIPTION OF MY EXPERIENCE ....
....
....
DATE SEEN ..../........./.........

BIRD ....
WHERE ....
DESCRIPTION OF MY EXPERIENCE ....
....
....
DATE SEEN ..../........./.........

PAGES FOR YOUR THOUGHTS

AND NOW WE COME TO THE GREAT, WIDE-OPEN WILDERNESS OF BLANK

PAGES FOR YOU TO ROAM OR RUN THE RAPIDS with words. Set up a narrative base camp site here, make this one giant bucket list, or fill with your poetry, prose, and praise about what you experience. Enjoy exploring and recording the known and unknowns.

166

MOOSE

BLACK BEAR
FRONT REAR

RED FOX
FRONT REAR

RACOON
FRONT REAR

NORTH AMERICAN
MAMMAL TRACKS

THE ART OF THE GREAT OUTDOORS

WHETHER YOU WANT TO DOODLE your delights and deeds or prepare to be an *en plein* painter (French for "in the open air"), here are some pages to serve as your portable canvas in the worldwide studio of nature. You may want to sketch some of your highlights, joining a long tradition of those who artfully depict their travels in their journals.

Sketching can help you hone your observations, be in the moment, and give your experiences lasting impressions. After making your marks on the pages, you may want to mix some watercolors with your favorite river or lake water, or try making your own colors from natural elements. Try pressing in some flowers or leaves.

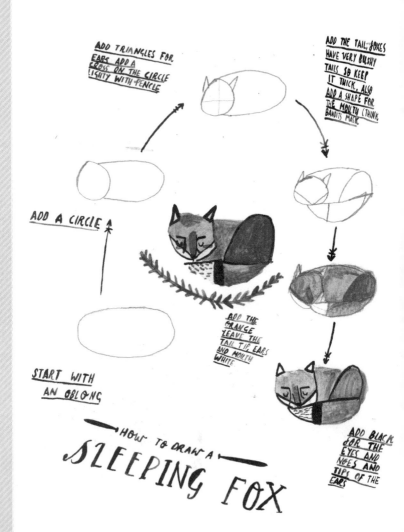

ADD TRIANGLES FOR EARS. ADD A CROSS ON THE CIRCLE LIGHTY WITH PENCIL

ADD THE TAIL, FOXES HAVE VERY BUSHY TAILS SO KEEP IT THICK. ALSO ADD A SHAPE FOR THE MOUTH (THINK BANDITS MASK)

ADD A CIRCLE

START WITH AN OBLONG

ADD THE ORANGE LEAVE THE TAIL TIP, EARS AND MOUTH WHITE

ADD BLACK FOR THE EYES AND NOSE AND TIPS OF THE EARS

HOW TO DRAW A SLEEPING FOX

SKETCHES

SKETCHES

HOW TO DRAW A
BLACK BEAR

START WITH AN
OVAL

THEN ADD A
CIRCLE

THEN ADD THE
LEGS * HINT
BEARS WALK
WITH THEIR LEGS
FACING INWARDS,
THIS GIVES THEM
AN AWKWARD
SWAGGER

ADD THE SHAPES
FOR THE INNER
EARS, EYES CHEST
PATCH & TOES

DRAW IN THE
EYES NOES &
MOUTH

ADD THE
EARS

COLOUR IN
BROWN AND
BLACK

SKETCHES

SKETCHES

SKETCHES

SKETCHES

SKETCHES

SKETCHES

SKETCHES

SKETCHES

SKETCHES

SKETCHES

SKETCHES

SKETCHES

SKETCHES

SKETCHES

SKETCHES

SKETCHES

SKETCHES

SKETCHES

ACKNOWLEDGMENTS

Sometimes the glories of the outdoors infuse one with gratitude. You want to shout "thank you!" into the canyon that echoes, or write *mahalo* (Hawaiian for "thank you") into the sand near the waterfall that cascades into the sea. Other times you want to whisper prayers of appreciation for escaping danger or witnessing wonder.

Thank you for holding this book and wanting to author your own experiences.

Heartfelt thanks to all those who keep the outdoors great.

Thanks to Jeffrey Kimball for creating the bird bucket lists and to Abbey Levantini for botanical garden ideas. For their destination suggestions, thanks to many outdoors lovers, including Dan Austin, Kasey Austin, Diane Bair, Alexandra Beezy, Jennifer Burnell, Sue Campbell, Jayne Clark, Yasue Haller, Krista Heinike, Craig Hilton, Peter Hughes, Steve Jermanok, Dan Leeth, Stephen Nowland, Kathy Spielman, Terry Zinn, and Dave Wiggins.

Thanks also to my parents. My childhood vacations involved houseboating on rivers and lakes, or sharing a cabin in Yosemite or a beach house with another family. And last, but never least, thanks to my husband, who shares moonrises from our backyard and far-flung places.

ABOUT THE AUTHOR

Award-winning writer, filmmaker, and photographer Lisa TE Sonne (www.LisaSonne.com) has also authored *My Adventures: A Traveler's Journal*, *The Happiness Handbook*, and *Everything 101: A Complete Education*. She has enjoyed the great outdoors on all seven continents and in many oceans.

ABOUT THE ILLUSTRATOR

Dick Vincent is an illustrator based in Manchester, UK. He is a cat owner and bread maker often found roaming the hills of Calderdale. Find more of his work on instagram @dickvincent or on Etsy at www.etsy.com/shop/dickvincent.